A Library of Modern Religious Thought

LESSING'S THEOLOGICAL WRITINGS

A LIBRARY OF
MODERN RELIGIOUS THOUGHT
General Editor: Henry Chadwick, D.D.

S. T. COLERIDGE
CONFESSIONS OF AN INQUIRING SPIRIT
Edited by H. StJ. Hart

LESSING'S THEOLOGICAL WRITINGS
Selected and translated by Henry Chadwick

DAVID HUME
THE NATURAL HISTORY OF RELIGION
Edited by H. E. Root

S. KIERKEGAARD
JOHANNES CLIMACUS and A SERMON
Translated and edited by T. H. Croxall

JOHN LOCKE
THE REASONABLENESS OF CHRISTIANITY
Edited and abridged by I. T. Ramsey

THE MIND OF
THE OXFORD MOVEMENT
Edited by Owen Chadwick

LESSING'S
THEOLOGICAL WRITINGS

Selections in translation
with an Introductory Essay
by
HENRY CHADWICK, B.D.
FELLOW OF QUEENS' COLLEGE, CAMBRIDGE

STANFORD UNIVERSITY PRESS
STANFORD, CALIFORNIA

Stanford University Press
Stanford, California
Copyright 1956 by A. and C. Black Ltd.
Printed in the United States of America
ISBN 0-8047-0335-3
Original American Edition 1957
Last figure below indicates year of this printing:
81 80 79 78 77 76 75 74 73 72

CONTENTS

PREFACE

The writings of Lessing translated in this book are intended to provide representative specimens of his mind for the use of students of theology and the history of ideas who may have insufficient German to read them in the original language. There exist in English valuable studies of Lessing as critic, poet, and dramatist, but they have less to say about his religious questionings. Theology was one of the major interests of his life, and his last decade was largely devoted to theological debate. His writings not only do much to illustrate the thought of the German Enlightenment. His treatment of the Gospels as historical documents begins to break new ground. He raises problems concerning revelation and history and concerning the difficulty of uncertainty in Christianity as a historical religion which have profoundly affected modern theology since his time. Paul Tillich has described modern apologetics as "answering theology." I venture to hope that this volume may prove useful to students of European religious thought since the eighteenth century who wish to investigate the background of some of the questions.

References to Lessing are to the edition of Lachmann and Muncker, 23 volumes, 1886–1924. I have also consulted that of Witkowski (Meyers Klassiker-Ausgaben). The translations are my own, except for *The Education of the Human Race*, which is a revision of that by F. W. Robertson (1858). The first English version of this work appeared in the *Monthly Repository of Theology and General Literature*, i (1806), pp. 412–20, 467–73, but attracted little notice, as appears from the comments in the same journal, New Series, iv (1830), pp. 300 ff. An American translation appeared in 1847 by F. H. Hedge, *Prose Writers of Germany* (revised edition, Philadelphia, 1870).

I have to thank Mrs. Helen Tomlinson for preparing the typescript. Dr. E. A. Blackall, Fellow of Gonville and Caius College, and Mr. M. J. D. Bown, lately scholar of Queens' College, have kindly allowed me to consult them over problems of Lessing's language. Errors remain my own.

H. C.

CAMBRIDGE,
October, 1954.

7

INTRODUCTION

I. THE OLD ORTHODOXY AND THE FRAGMENTS OF REIMARUS

Gotthold Ephraim Lessing was born in 1729 at Kamenz in the Electorate of Saxony. He was the son of an orthodox Lutheran pastor with strong academic and intellectual interests, and in 1746 was sent to the University of Leipzig to study theology. His all-absorbing interest rapidly became the stage, and it was not long before he gained permission from his father to abandon theology. Debt forced him to give up his university studies, and in 1749 he went to Berlin, where he met some of the more advanced representatives of the German Enlightenment such as Nicolai and the Jew Moses Mendelssohn, who became his close friends. In 1755 he moved to Leipzig for three years, returning to Berlin in 1758. In 1760 he moved to Breslau, where he wrote the comedy *Minna von Barnhelm* and his æsthetic study *Laocoon*. During his five years at Breslau he began to collect his library, particularly studying Leibniz, Spinoza, and the early Church Fathers. In 1765 he visited Berlin, hoping (in vain) for the post of Royal Librarian. In 1766 he found congenial work as consultant and dramatic critic to the recently founded theatre at Hamburg. But a financial deficit soon brought the theatre to an end. In 1769 Lessing was offered the post of librarian at the Duke of Brunswick's library at Wolfenbüttel. Here at last he had security and full opportunity to pursue the theological and scholarly interests which had been asserting themselves in the background of his mind.[1]

The first of his published writings on theology is the *Vindication of Hieronymus Cardanus*, 1754. Jerome Cardan of Milan, philosopher of the Italian Renaissance, was accused of atheism on account of his work *de Subtilitate*, 1552, in which he had ventured to compare Christianity with Judaism, Islam, and paganism. Lessing's argument runs that

[1] In December 1757 he wrote to Moses Mendelssohn: "Only a part of our youth should be given to the fine arts; we have to exercise ourselves in more important matters before we die" (Lachmann-Muncker, *Lessings Werke*, xvii, pp. 130–1).

Cardan must in fact have been a loyal Christian since he suppresses the most cogent arguments in favour of the other religions, especially Islam. As arguments in favour of Christianity Cardan brings forward the three traditional "historical" arguments: the fulfilment of Old Testament prophecy in the life of Jesus, the miracles that he did, and the amazing expansion of Christianity in the ancient world. His fourth argument is that Jesus' ethical teaching is identical with that of natural morality. But Cardan neglects the strong case that might be put by a Moslem. Such a man could reasonably urge that Judaism and Christianity claim revelations superior to reason, the possibility of which they are unable to demonstrate. They assert "mysteries," and so leave the door open for all manner of superstition. Islam, on the other hand, has no doctrine not in accord with reason. Moslems believe in one God, and in retribution in a future life. If Christians believe that God requires more of man than virtue, the *onus probandi* is on them. Moslems make no extravagant assertions that their prophet rose from the dead and said "I am son of God," and make no appeal to miracles.[1] In short, Lessing suggests, Cardan was unfair in his comparison of religions; for the superiority of Christianity over Islam depends precisely upon the validity of the historical arguments for Christianity which had been undermined by the English deists.

He published at the same time a *Vindication of the Ineptus Religiosus*, which is a proof of the orthodox origin of a seventeenth-century book, consisting of aphorisms of advice on religion written with a subtle irony, which had been censured as "an evil and godless little book" by Pastor Johann Vogt in his *Catalogus historico-criticus librorum rariorum* (Hamburg, 1732).

Vindication was a favourite interest of Lessing. In his first year at Wolfenbüttel he found in the library a manuscript containing a reply to Lanfranc by Berengar of Tours. He saw that this reply rendered necessary a revaluation of the heretic, which he wrote in 1770. His concern is for a just historical estimate. Historical writing must be set free from propaganda and from the prejudice of dogmatic assumptions. For theological reasons his *Berengarius Turonensis* received a warm

---

[1] For the accord between Islamic doctrine and natural theology cf. Leibniz, *Theodicy*, preface (ed. A. Farrer, 1952, p. 51); Thomas Woolston, *Third Discourse on the Miracles of our Saviour* (1728), p. 66: "Mahometanism . . . is a more reasonable Religion than the Christian, upon modern Schemes and Systems."

welcome from orthodox Lutherans,[1] though on that account less orthodox theologians and his enlightened friends at Berlin regarded these excursions into theology with anxiety.[2] In 1773 Lessing began to publish a series of *Contributions to Literature and History from the Ducal Library at Wolfenbüttel* (by a decision of 13 February 1772 the Duke of Brunswick exempted Lessing from censorship in this series, provided that he did not attack religion). In the first part he published an unprinted comment of Leibniz on the pains of hell, in which Leibniz defended the doctrine against the criticism of Ernst Soner (1572–1612), Professor of Medicine at Altorf and a secret Socinian. Leibniz is shown not merely to have defended the doctrine in public while denying it in private (though Lessing would have thought none the worse of him had it been so); he defended the orthodox doctrine because it was nearer the truth than the opposite standpoint of the Socinians. Lessing goes on to take up a critique of Leibniz's view by the liberal theologian of Halle, J. A. Eberhard (1738–1809), who in his *New Apology of Socrates* (1772) had attacked as inhuman the idea that all the heathen will burn for ever. In the orthodox doctrine of eternal punishment Lessing sees enshrined the truth that "nothing in the world is isolated, nothing is without consequences, nothing without eternal consequences." Hell is another name for the natural consequences of sin. Its sufferings are relative and can be remedial, a means towards the restoration of perfection. Heaven and hell must be seen to be relative and not absolute states. In the best man there is much evil, and in the worst some good. The consequences of evil must remain with the good even in heaven, and those of good with the wicked even in hell. Heaven and hell have gradations and degrees which one can pass through. The neology of Halle tries to get rid of hell. These modern theologians would do better if they could eliminate the notion that heaven and hell are absolutes, and see them as constituting a continuum and as both alike a process of purification.

The essay *Leibniz on Eternal Punishments* made a profound impression upon Lessing's contemporaries. It admirably illustrates the acuteness of his mind, and the ingenuity of his tactics in theological debate. A superficial reader with orthodox beliefs might be pleased

---

[1] Lessing's letter to Eva König, 25 Oct. 1770, expresses cynical pleasure at this reception.
[2] Letter from his brother Karl, 4 June 1771.

with his apparent defence of traditional doctrine and proof that Leibniz upheld it. He would certainly welcome the attack on the popular "liberalism" of Eberhard. But while Lessing has indeed made palpable hits on the neology of Halle, he can scarcely be said to have given support to orthodoxy, since *inter alia* he has virtually eliminated the idea of the supernatural, at least as that idea was traditionally understood, and interprets both heaven and hell as a purgatory.

A similar plea for Trinitarian orthodoxy as defended by Leibniz, accompanied by a tendency to treat Socinian and liberalizing opinions with scorn, appears in his essay of 1773, *The Objections of Andreas Wissowatius against the Trinity*, in which Lessing states the objections raised by a Socinian contemporary of Leibniz and the reply which that philosopher made to him.

In the third part of his *Contributions* in 1774 he printed a study entitled *Of Adam Neuser: some Authentic Accounts*. Neuser, a Lutheran who turned Calvinist, was accused in 1572 with three others of denying the Trinity and the divinity of Christ, and was imprisoned. One of them, Sylvanus, was executed on charges of blasphemy and treason; the other two recanted and were exiled. Neuser himself escaped to Constantinople, where he was forced to become a Moslem, and died in 1576. Traditionally he had been represented as a wicked heretic and apostate. Lessing tells his story with compassion, representing him as a poor man forced into apostasy by the fanaticism of the orthodox theologians of Heidelberg, as yet another Servetus, and as an honest man who with more logic and deeper sincerity than the Socinians (and, it is implied, the neology of Lessing's time) drew from his denial of the divinity of Christ the not unreasonable conclusion that prayer might not be directed to him.

These examples of Lessing's method show him apparently supporting orthodoxy against Socinianism and modern "enlightened" Christianity. But there is discernible a subtle undercurrent in the argument. His public upholding of orthodoxy is not to be taken at its face value. Even Lessing's friends were deceived by him, and the Berlin Enlightenment at first regarded him with as much alarm as the orthodox with pleasure. A letter of 2 February 1774 to his brother Karl, who at first could not understand how his enlightened brother Gotthold could have gone back to study theology instead of writing plays, reveals his tactics:

"With orthodoxy, thank God, there was a tolerably clear understanding. A curtain had been drawn between it and philosophy [i.e. by Liebniz], behind which each could go its own way without interfering with the other. But what is happening now ? This curtain is being torn down, and under the pretext of making us reasonable Christians we are turned into extremely unreasonable philosophers. I beseech you, dear brother, look rather less at what our modern theologians discard than at what they want to put in its place. We are one in our conviction that our old religious system is false. But I cannot say with you that it is a patchwork of bunglers and half-philosophers. I know of nothing in the world upon the study of which human intelligence has been more acutely shown and exercised. What really is a patchwork of bunglers and half-philosophers is the religious system which they now want to put in place of the old ; and with far more influence upon reason and philosophy than the old arrogated to itself."

Lessing's plan is to clear out of the way the neology of J. S. Semler and the Halle theologians, to make room for a radical upheaval of the old religion. The liberal theologians said "Peace, peace" when there was no peace. Semler's great work of scholarship, *A Free Investigation of the Canon* (1771-75), only aroused his scorn. On 11 November 1774 he wrote acidly to his brother that he intended to publish an even freer investigation of the Canon. Orthodoxy must· be supported in order to make its downfall possible. The liberal theology of Semler and his school was deceptively credible. Orthodoxy was patently absurd, and should be upheld in order to hasten its destruction.

Lessing's cynicism re-emerges in two letters of 1777. On 20 March he wrote to his brother, again defending his turn from the theatre to theology, which Karl regarded as eccentric and regrettable, and particularly defending his Counter-propositions to Reimarus (see below), which Karl thought would merely prop up hoary irrationalities :

"I only prefer the old orthodox theology (at bottom, tolerant) to the new (at bottom, intolerant) because the former is in manifest conflict with human reason, whereas the latter might easily take one in. I make agreement with my obvious enemies in order to be able to be the better on my guard against my secret adversaries."

On 25 May he wrote again to Karl that "if the world must be kept going with untruths, then the old which are already practicable[1] are just as good as new ones."

Lessing was well aware that by presenting his arguments in the form of historical studies he gave them an air of academic detachment which could protect him from attack. And he knew that there is a difference between telling the whole truth and telling nothing but the truth. The introduction to his *Berengarius Turonensis* contains a characteristic comment in reply to a suggestion of the learned historian J. L. Mosheim that Berengar's eucharistic theology could not now be known, since to escape condemnation he had expressed himself with deliberate obscurity. Lessing counters: "I do not know whether it is a duty to sacrifice life and fortune for truth; at least the courage and resolution needed for this are not gifts that we can give to ourselves." A writer, he continues, is only under an obligation where he does tell the truth to tell fully and frankly and not to present a garbled mixture of truth and falsehood, the detection of which is much more difficult than mere lies.[2]

With the principle of reserve in the communication of irreligious knowledge Lessing had much sympathy. During his stay at Hamburg he had made the acquaintance of the family of Hermann Samuel Reimarus, a Professor of Oriental Languages, who died in 1769, leaving in the hands of his daughter Elise an enormous unpublished work entitled *Apology for Rational Worshippers of God*.[3] Elise passed it to Lessing, who, rightly judging that on account of both dimensions and content the whole was unprintable, decided that

---

[1] Lessing valued traditional Christian dogmas because, although mistaken, they produced practical conduct of which he approved; cf. the end of *The Proof of the Spirit and of Power*, and the exaltation of conduct over theological speculations in *Thoughts on the Moravians*.

[2] Lachmann-Muncker, xi, pp. 69–70, Cf. Kant, *Religion innerhalb der Grenzen der blossen Vernunft*, IV, ii, 4 (note at end of section), who distinguishes between *Offenherzigkeit*, which is to utter all the truth one knows, and *Aufrichtigkeit*, which only means that everything that one utters is true; the former, he says, is not to be expected, but the latter can be demanded of everyone (Hartenstein's ed., V, p. 289).

[3] The fullest account of this long dissertation is given in D. F. Strauss, *H. S. Reimarus und seine Schutzschrift für die vernünftigen Verehrer Gottes* (1862). Although Reimarus was at once rumoured to be a possible author, there were many other speculations, and it was not certainly known until 1814.

anonymous fragments should appear in instalments in his *Contributions to Literature and History*, where he was safe from the censor.[1]

The first fragment appeared in 1774 (with *Adam Neuser*), entitled by Lessing "On the Toleration of the Deists: fragment of an anonymous writer." He provided a disingenuous preface containing the assertion, "I have been quite unable to discover how and when it came into our Library," and in an attempt to put the witch-hunters on to a false scent suggested that the author might be J. Lorenz Schmidt (1702–49). Schmidt was a deist who in 1735 published a free translation of the Pentateuch with rationalist notes; the resulting furore led to his arrest. The last ten years of his life were lived in obscurity under assumed names, though he was able to produce a German translation of Matthew Tindal's *Christianity as Old as the Creation* in 1741, and the first translation of Spinoza's *Ethics*, disguised as a refutation of that "atheist," in 1744. He was offered asylum by the Duke of Brunswick and died in humiliation at Wolfenbüttel. From this unhappy story Lessing learnt that it could be dangerous to reveal one's true opinion.

Reimarus' first fragment affirms that since Jesus was a teacher of rational, practical religion, anyone who is rational and follows his practical ethical teaching may entitle himself a Christian. But the simplicity of Christ's teaching has been tragically corrupted. The apostles, with their Jewish ideas of the Messiah and the divine inspiration of the Hebrew scriptures, produced an entirely different system full of mysteries. And now, though Jews and pagans are tolerated, deists are not. Rationalists ought to be accorded the same toleration as God commanded the ancient Israelites to grant to the stranger within the gates.

The fragment attracted little notice. And in 1777 Lessing made bold to print five further instalments.

The first of these, entitled "Of the Decrying of Reason in the Pulpit," argues that since only reason can prove the truth of the Christian faith, the clergy are ill-advised to disparage it; they are only cutting off the branch on which they sit.[2]

---

[1] Lessing's respect for his father no doubt helped to restrain him before he arrived at Wolfenbüttel. But his father's death in 1770 and the exemption from censorship gave him a freedom he had not before felt himself to possess.

[2] The Savoyard priest in Rousseau's *Émile* puts the same point: "He who denies the right of reason must convince me without recourse to her aid" (Everyman ed., p. 265).

The second is more important, and is headed "Impossibility of a Revelation which All Men can Believe on Rational Grounds." Here Reimarus argues that God cannot make special revelations to everybody, since the continuous succession of miracles would disrupt the natural order, and God would be contradicting himself. Therefore, if revelation is to occur at all, it can only occur on rare occasions and to particular individuals, in whose testimony other men must put their trust. To these others there is no direct revelation, only human testimony concerning revelation. Because men can be deceived and deceiving, there is no safe guarantee of divine revelation. By some the testimony may be found credible, but not by others. This element of uncertainty is enormously magnified if the revelation is claimed to have occurred in remote antiquity. As the testimony passes from mouth to mouth, it loses more and more reliability. Moreover, comparatively few have any chance to believe even this indirect testimony. Many die in early youth before they are of age to comprehend it. And the vast majority of mankind have never heard of it at all. Christian missionaries have done little, though admittedly that little has been at great sacrifice to the individuals concerned. But Christian Spaniards murdered forty million men in America. The Americans would scarcely regard them as bringers of a divine revelation. Most of those who travel to foreign lands go to exploit the natives. The alleged revelation has done little to mitigate their cupidities. It would be better to call off the missionary movement and leave Moslems, Confucianists, and Jews to themselves. Furthermore, the revelation (for Reimarus equivalent to an infallible Bible) is interpreted so variously. Each commentator finds his own doctrine therein, Roman, Lutheran, Calvinist, and Arminian. And this Bible is open to criticism; to regard Moses as author of the Pentateuch is absurd. The apostles' writings are occasional productions; they were never intended to be the vehicle of revealed dogmas; much that they wrote has been lost (and how could God have allowed his absolute revelations to be lost?). In short, special revelation is out of the question. Salvation is through the book of nature, by the natural religion of all men of all ages and all places— "quod ubique, quod semper, quod ab omnibus."[1]

The third fragment, "The Passage of the Israelites through the Red Sea," points out the startling difficulties involved in the story (Exodus

[1] Rousseau's Savoyard priest argues similarly (*loc. cit.*, pp. 260 ff.).

xii. 37 ff.) that six hundred thousand men of war, besides their families and stuff, all passed through the Red Sea in a single night. Reimarus calculates that if there were so many fighting men, the numbers of the entire nation must have been three million, one fighting man to every four others. There were also animals; say, three hundred thousand oxen and cows, six hundred thousand sheep and goats, etc. If the Israelites moved in a column, ten deep, the length of the column would have been one hundred and eighty miles, and they would have taken nine days to cross as a minimum figure.

The fourth fragment argues "That the Books of the Old Testament were Not Written to Reveal a Religion," on the ground that they contain no doctrine of a future life. The immortality of the soul was recognized to be a truth of natural religion; if the Old Testament said nothing about it, this would seriously prejudice its claim to instruct mankind in religious truth.

The fifth fragment, "On the Resurrection Narrative," analyses the inconsistencies among the evangelists, and concludes that since they disagree about the detailed circumstances they are altogether mistaken about the fact.

At the end of all Lessing appends his own "Editor's Counter-propositions":

"And now enough of these fragments. Any of my readers who would prefer me to have spared them altogether is surely more timid than well instructed. He may be a very devout Christian, but he is certainly not a very enlightened one. He may be wholehearted in his upholding of his religion; but he ought also to have greater confidence in it.

"For how much could be said in reply to all these objections and difficulties! And even if absolutely no answer were forthcoming, what then? The learned theologian might in the last resort be embarrassed, but certainly not the Christian. To the former it might at most cause confusion to see the supports with which he would uphold religion shattered in this way, to find the buttresses cast down by which, God willing, he would have made it safe and sound. But how do this man's hypotheses, explanations, and proofs affect the Christian? For him it is simply a fact—the Christianity which he feels to be true and in which he feels blessed. When the paralytic feels the beneficial shocks of the electric spark, does it worry him whether Nollet or Franklin or neither of them is right?

"In short, the letter is not the spirit, and the Bible is not religion. Consequently, objections to the letter and to the Bible are not also objections to the spirit and to religion.

"For the Bible obviously contains more than is essential to religion, and it is a mere hypothesis to assert that it must be equally infallible in this excess of matter. Moreover, religion was there before a Bible existed. Christianity was there before the evangelists and apostles wrote. A long period elapsed before the first of them wrote, and a very considerable time before the entire canon was complete. Therefore while much may depend upon these writings, it is impossible to suppose that the entire truth of the religion depends upon them. If there was a period in which it had already spread far and in which it had gained many souls, and when, nevertheless, not a letter of that which has come down to us had yet been written down, then it must also be possible that everything which the evangelists and apostles wrote could have been lost, and yet that the religion which they taught would have continued. The religion is not true because the evangelists and apostles taught it; but they taught it because it is true.[1] The written traditions must be interpreted by their inward truth and no written traditions can give the religion any inward truth if it has none.

"This, therefore, would be the general answer to a large part of these fragments, as I have said, in the worst case."

Lessing is evidently anxious that in the inevitable explosion that must follow on the publication of the fragments the laity may be kept out of the fight by his reassurances. The battle will be far easier for him if he has only the clergy to deal with, for then he can probably persuade the liberal and orthodox theologians to start a fight among themselves so that they do not unite in an onslaught upon him.

After his preliminary generalities he proceeds to comment in more detail upon Reimarus' main points. So far from decrying reason contemporary liberal preachers were continually emphasizing "the inner link between reason and faith." They say:

[1] Cf. Matthew Tindal, *Christianity as Old as the Creation* (1730), p. 336: "The Christian Deists . . . believe not the Doctrines because contain'd in Scripture, but the Scripture on account of the Doctrines."

"Faith is reason strengthened by miracles and signs, and reason is faith made reasonable. The whole of revealed religion is simply a renewed sanction of the religion of reason. Either there are no mysteries in it at all or, if there are such, it is a matter of indifference whether the Christian connects with them this or that concept or even none at all."

For such preachers Lessing has only contempt. The laity are not to be led astray by them, but may take heart from the platitude that in the controversy between reason and revelation "the truth lies where it always lies, between two extremes." Only reason can decide about the possibility and claims of revelation. But if its decision is favourable, then reason must be

"yet another argument for the truth of revelation rather than an objection to it if it finds things in it which transcend its power of conception. Anyone who refines such things out of his religion has as good as no religion at all. For what is a revelation which reveals nothing? Is it enough to preserve the mere name though the thing has already been discarded?"

On the contrary, "revealed religion does not in the least presuppose a rational religion" in the sense that without it it is unintelligible, but rather "includes it within itself"; that is to say, "it contains all the truths which reason teaches but merely supports them with a different sort of argument."

Reimarus' second fragment is to be answered by the simple statement: "That revelation is necessary for salvation even for those men who have never attained to any knowledge of it at all, or at any rate any rational knowledge of it, is not the teaching of Christ, nor has it ever been the generally recognized teaching of the Church." Reimarus has failed to distinguish between the statements of Christ and those of some ill-instructed Christian handbook, and treats both as if they were on the same level.

The criticism of the Old Testament in the fourth fragment reckons without the idea of progress in history. To his comments Lessing appends, as if it were the work of someone else, the first fifty-three paragraphs of his work *The Education of the Human Race*, the whole of which appeared in 1780.[1]

[1] On 25 February 1780 he wrote to his brother Karl that he now felt able to

Commenting on the analysis of the discrepancies between the Gospel narratives of the resurrection Lessing observes that the evangelists were not the same people as those who actually witnessed the resurrection; therefore, a distinction must be drawn between contradictions among the witnesses and contradictions among the evangelists. And even if there do appear to be instances of the former, that is only to be expected. Experience shows how eyewitnesses of any given event will give surprisingly different accounts of it, and how even one and the same person repeating his account of an event at various times will tell his story in different ways.

The last argument was not so commonplace in the eighteenth century as it may now appear. For it presupposes the abandonment of the traditional orthodox idea that the evangelists were wholly preserved from error by supernatural inspiration. Here Lessing's apologetic, considered merely as an argument, was an immeasurably stronger reply to Reimarus than anything that could be provided from the arsenal of orthodoxy (whether Protestant or Roman). Because Lessing could not believe the traditional idea of revelation, he was able to read the Bible like any other book. In the seventeenth-century tract defended by him in the *Vindication of the Ineptus Religiosus* there occur the words: "Read the Bible just as you read Livy."[1] Because Lessing did so, he was able to raise without embarrassment or prejudice the question of the sources of the Gospels. The *New Hypothesis concerning the Evangelists regarded as merely human Historians*, composed in 1777–78, was regarded by Lessing not only as his best work in the field of theological inquiry, but also as a more formidable attack on traditional orthodoxy than anything else he had written.[2] The controversy concerning the fragments of Reimarus became so intense that he had to defer his intention of printing it, and it first appeared in 1784,

publish the whole of it, "since I shall never acknowledge it to be my own work." That Lessing wrote the whole, and that the old view, advanced by Körte (1839) and G. Krüger (1913), attributing at least the first fifty-three sections, and perhaps the whole, to Albrecht Thaer is untenable, has been finally shown by A. M. Wagner, "Who is the Author of Lessing's 'Education of Mankind'?", in *Modern Language Review*, xxxviii (1943), pp. 318–27, and H. Schneider, *Lessing* (Bern, 1951), pp. 222–30.

[1] Lachmann-Muncker, v, p. 340. Cf. John Toland, *Christianity Not Mysterious*, II, iii, 22 (1702 edn., p. 49): "Nor is there any different Rule to be follow'd in the Interpretation of Scripture from what is common to all other Books."

[2] Letter to his brother Karl of 25 February 1778.

edited by his brother Karl. There is no doubt that he was right in thinking it his most solid contribution to the advancement of learning. He treats the first three Gospels as documents falling into a quite separate category from the fourth. The fourth Gospel, he thinks, contains a very different notion of the person of Christ, and was intended to provide a theological basis for the Gentile Christian church at the stage of its development when it was breaking free from its Palestinian origins. The first three Gospels, on the other hand, do not contain a doctrine of the person of Christ that demands more than that he was an inspired, wonder-working man, the true, promised Messiah; and they are much more closely connected with Judaism. And the literary phenomena are to be thus explained: the evangelists all drew upon an original Aramaic Gospel which contained the immediate reminiscences of the apostles, which was preserved among the Jewish Christians and their successors, the later Ebionites. This document possessed by the Ebionite congregations was called by the Church Fathers the Gospel according to the Hebrews, or Gospel of the Nazarenes. Although Lessing's literary hypothesis lacks a sound historical and critical basis, his work is the first of the long series of studies in the Gospels which have begun from his theological starting-point in placing the fourth Gospel in a category by itself. And he perceived that, before there could be any adequate discussion of the questions put by Reimarus concerning the historical Jesus, there must be a preliminary critical investigation of the sources.

If he was disappointed at provoking little reaction with the fragment "On the Toleration of the Deists" of 1774, he was rewarded by the response to the five fragments of 1777. There was a general mobilization of the orthodox. First came a polite and respectful reply from J. D. Schumann of Hanover, On the Evidence of the Proofs of the Truth of the Christian Religion, which restated the traditional "historical" arguments of miracle and prophecy. This drew from Lessing the famous pamphlet On the Proof of the Spirit and of Power, with the appended Testament of John. The Lutheran superintendent at Wolfenbüttel, J. H. Ress, published anonymously a Defence of the Story of the Resurrection of Jesus Christ, in which he attempted to harmonize the Gospel narratives. This provoked Lessing to a long Rejoinder (Eine Duplik), written in a somewhat exasperated and sarcastic tone. Both Schumann and Ress tried to answer Reimarus. But the main defence of the traditional view of scripture was to come from Johann Melchior Goeze (1717–86), pastor of the Lutheran Church of St. Catharine at Hamburg. During Lessing's stay at Hamburg Goeze had been on friendly terms with him; but some estrangement followed Lessing's failure to reply to questions from Goeze concerning old Bibles in the Wolfenbüttel library. Goeze's attack is directed not against Reimarus but against Lessing himself. Since most of the books on this controversy tell the story from Lessing's point of view, and take him as the hero, Goeze is usually represented as a stupid obscurantist. It must be granted that he cannot compete with Lessing as a master of the art of invective. Perhaps in that art Lessing's only serious rival in all literature is Saint Jerome. But if we do not read Goeze through Lessing's spectacles,[1] we find a sincere and compassionate pastor of his flock, not without some claim to learning, who seeks to protect his people from disturbing doubts and questionings with which they are ill-equipped to deal. The justification of Goeze lies in his well-founded belief that the fragments of Reimarus are upsetting simple believers. Lessing has made a subject, which ought properly to be discussed calmly in private among the learned, a matter for general debate in the public streets. He ought to have published Reimarus, if at all, in the decent obscurity of a Latin translation. (It is intelligible that for this Lessing charged him with Romanizing.)[2]

On 24 December 1777 Lessing's wife Eva, whom he had married in October 1776, gave birth to a child which died within a few hours; and she died on 10 January 1788. In loneliness and bitterness of soul Lessing flung himself into the controversy with Goeze.

His first reply is entitled *A Parable*. A wise king once possessed a vast

[1] His attacks on Lessing are collected by E. Schmidt, *Goezes Streitschriften gegen Lessing* (Stuttgart, 1893).

[2] Compare J. H. Newman's view that the liberal Anglican manifesto *Essays and Reviews* (1860) was wrong not in content but in form. Its error, he told Mark Pattison in conversation, lay in "the throwing of such speculations broadcast upon the general public. It was . . . unsettling their faith without offering them anything else to rest upon. But he had no word of censure for the latitude of theological speculation assumed by the essay [i.e. that contributed by Pattison], provided it had been addressed *ad clerum*, or put out, not as a public appeal, but as a scholastic dissertation addressed to learned theologians. He assured me that this could be done in the Roman communion, and that much greater latitude of speculation on theological topics was allowed in this form in the Catholic Church than in Protestant communities" (M. Pattison, *Memoirs*, 1885, pp. 316 f.).

and noble palace, the architecture of which was eccentric and conflicted with all the accepted canons of style.[1] Yet it lasted well and was convenient. Looked at from outside it appeared to some extent unintelligible, but from within it was full of light, and its design seemed consistent. Numerous connoisseurs of architecture claimed to possess the plans of the original architects, which were marked with obscure words in a language now lost; each of them took it upon himself to improve it in accordance with his own interpretation of these obscure markings. There were, however, a few who said: "What are your plans to us? Whether this or that, it is all the same. It is enough that at every moment we learn that the most beneficent wisdom fills the entire palace, and that from this source nothing but beauty and order are spread over the whole land." But there came a night when the rival contestants were all asleep and the watchmen shouted: "Fire! Fire in the palace!" The first thought of each was to save not the palace but his own plan, and in the resulting confusion they fell squabbling among themselves. The palace would indeed have been burnt down if there had been a real fire. But the frightened watchmen had mistaken a northern light for a conflagration.

Lessing's allegory needs no explication. He appended to it a request that Goeze should publicly withdraw his statement that Lessing had deliberately intended to attack Christianity by printing the fragments, and a challenge to carry on the debate which is remarkable not only because it reveals Lessing's stern determination to break the conspiracy of silence regarding critical matters, but also because he here claims that the right to protest against the shackles of tradition is vindicated by the high example of Luther. This powerful plea he was to repeat later: "The true Lutheran does not wish to be defended by Luther's writings but by Luther's spirit; and Luther's spirit absolutely requires that no man may be prevented from advancing in the knowledge of the truth according to his own judgment."[2]

With this claim Lessing imported into German Protestantism and many history books the legend that the fundamental principle of the Reformation was the right to exercise unrestricted private judgment. The legend was not entirely his invention, since there are plentiful

[1] For God as "like an architect of a lovely palace," cf. Leibniz, *Theodicy*, i, 78.
[2] Lessing, *Anti-Goeze*, I. It appears again in *Anti-Goeze*, X. Cf. H. Bornkamm, *Luther im Spiegel der deutschen Geistesgeschichte* (1955), pp. 14 f.

anticipations in the English deists and in Semler. It is a claim which has had enormous effects on the European mind, among others the ease with which all non-Roman dogmatic theology can be caricatured as a collection of interesting private opinions, or even prejudices, which the individual holds because he happens to think them probable rather than because he receives them on any supernatural authority.[1]

Because of his pastoral concern Goeze saw in Lessing's "Editorial Counter-propositions" a far more serious danger to his flock than in a dozen fragments of Reimarus. Lessing's reassurances to the laity might deceive the very elect. He drew from Lessing a vindication of the Counter-propositions entitled *Axioms, if there are Any in such Matters*, in which, to describe Goeze's position, he coined the word "Bibliolatry." The controversy now became a running fight, and Lessing published a series of eleven violent articles under the title *Anti-Goeze*.[2] This pamphlet war generated more heat than light, and the *Anti-Goeze* papers, though brilliantly written, do little to illuminate either Lessing's thought or the real issues at stake. It is mere theological Billingsgate. The *Axioms*, however, provoked Goeze to make a baffled request that Lessing should explain what he understood by the Christian religion when he declared that it could exist if the Bible were lost or had never been written.[3] He received in reply *G. E. Lessing's Necessary Answer to a very Unnecessary Question of Herr Hauptpastor Goeze in Hamburg*. Goeze expected him to declare himself; he believed him to be a deist who believed only in "natural religion," and was a disciple of Toland and Tindal.[4] Lessing was too clever to give any confession of faith. He replies that "by the Christian religion I understand all those doctrines which are contained in the creeds of the first four centuries of the Christian church," ironically adding that he would include the so-called Apostles' creed and the so-called Athanasian creed.[5] He has

---

[1] Cf. the cautionary tale of Erik Peterson's correspondence with Adolf Harnack, reprinted in Peterson's *Theologische Traktate* (Munich, 1950), pp. 293–321.

[2] Lessing's *Parable, Axioms,* and *Anti-Goeze* have been translated into English by H. H. Bernard, *Cambridge Free Thoughts and Letters on Bibliolatry* (London, 1862). The translator enlivens the text with anti-clerical notes which make this book something of a museum piece; it is only a pity that he omits passages (usually without indication) if he thinks them either irrelevant or too close to orthodoxy.

[3] Goeze, *Streitschriften*, pp. 68–9, ed. Schmidt.

[4] *Ibid.*, p. 166.

[5] It is a cliché of argument at this period that none of the three classical creeds,

avoided a decisive statement by giving a purely historical answer. Goeze at least realized, as Schumann and Ress did not, that the real enemy of orthodoxy was Lessing himself, and that his opponent was a very clever and elusive antagonist. The manner in which Lessing conducts his polemic is designed to conceal his true opinions. On 16 March 1778 he writes to his brother: "I must aim my weapons at my opponent; not all that I write γυμναστικῶς would I also write δογματικῶς."[1] And a letter to Elise Reimarus of 9 August 1778, soon after the publication of the *Necessary Answer*, explicitly reveals that Lessing has his tongue in his cheek:

> "I am delighted that you understand so well the tactics of my last pamphlet. . . . Since he has made the tactical error of wishing to know not what I believe of the the Christian religion but what I understand by the Christian religion, I have scored a victory, and the one half of Christendom must defend me in my fortification against the other half. Thus Paul divided the Sanhedrin, and I need only try to prevent . . . the Papists from becoming Lutherans and the Lutherans Papists."

In 1778 he poured fuel on the flames by publishing the longest and much the most formidable of Reimarus' fragments: "On the Intentions of Jesus and His Disciples."[2] The fragment draws a distinction between the beliefs and intentions of Jesus and those of the apostolic church. Jesus never intended to teach complicated dogmatic theology, the Trinity, the divine Sonship, the sacraments, and the rest. Matt. v. 17 ff. and xxiii. 3 f. show that he never intended his disciples not to continue observing the Jewish ceremonial law. His preaching has only a limited reference, and his ideas and language about the kingdom of God are purely those of Jewish apocalyptic. Jesus accepted the fanatical Jewish expectation of a Messianic deliverer from foreign domination, and dreamt that God would help him to achieve this end. But it was only a

Apostles', Nicene, or Athanasian, was composed by the author to whom it is attributed by tradition; cf. Antony Collins, *A Discourse of Free Thinking* (1713), p. 76.

[1] Is this a reminiscence of Athanasius' comment on Origen (*de Decretis*, 27)?

[2] There exists an English translation of the second part of the fragment by C. Voysey, *Fragments from Reimarus* (1879). Naturally the fragment has been congenial reading to the school of Albert Schweitzer; see his glowing appreciation in *The Quest of the Historical Jesus* (1910), pp. 15 ff.

dream, and the cry of dereliction on the cross expresses his disillusion-
ment. Admittedly there are passages in the Gospels which do not fit
this reading of the story. But these passages are to be explained as
insertions of the apostolic church. The apostles came to have intentions
very different from those of Jesus. The church developed the doctrine
that through his death Jesus atoned for sin, and entered into glory by
the resurrection, soon to return in judgment to condemn all who do not
believe in him. This belief became the foundation of the church's separation from Judaism, never intended by Jesus himself. Once these beliefs
had been formed, the church had to revise and interpolate the Gospels
to make them harmonize with their dogmas.

Reimarus is confident that he has rediscovered the Jesus of history,
overlaid by the accretions of the early church. He was a fanatical
Jewish peasant of somewhat limited intelligence, and certainly had no
ideas of a world-wide church of those who believe in his atoning death
and glorious resurrection. Knowing this (apparently a priori) Reimarus
has a criterion for disentangling the true traditions about the historical
Jesus from the beliefs of the apostolic church.

On 13 July 1778 (while the Necessary Answer was passing through
the press) Lessing was informed by the Duke of Brunswick that in
future all his writings on religion would be subject to the censor. This
was a decision deeply resented by Lessing; it brought to a stop the
spate of vituperative pamphlets against the poor Goeze. Checked by
authority, Lessing turned to the plan of putting his theology into a play
which would "play the theologians a still more annoying trick than
ten fragments." He would return to his "former pulpit, the theatre."[1]

The play Nathan the Wise (1779) is a plea for the toleration of all
religions (except the intolerant). The main characters are Nathan the
Jew, Saladin the Moslem, and the Knight Templar who represents
Christianity of the type Lessing would wish to encourage. Nathan is a
model of tolerant charity.[2] Saladin is runner-up. The Knight Templar,
though a fine character, is a Christian and has to learn as the play
proceeds to appreciate the virtue of religious indifferentism and the
vice of anti-semitism. The message of the play is that all men should

---

[1] Letter to his brother Karl, 11 August 1778. To the end Lessing had no
regrets whatever about having published the fragments of Reimarus (cf. the note
printed in Lachmann-Muncker, xvi, pp. 526–7).
[2] Nathan's character is intended to reflect his enlightened friend Mendelssohn.

treat one another as brothers, irrespective of their religious allegiance. Men are men before they are Christians, Jews, or Moslems. They have one and the same God as their universal Father.

The climax of the play comes in Act III, scene vii, in a dialogue between Nathan and Saladin (the Knight Templar is, perhaps significantly, absent), where Lessing uses a story from the *Decameron* of Boccaccio. Saladin puts to Nathan the question which of the three religions is true. Nathan replies with an allegory. An ancient Oriental possessed a priceless ring which had the power to render its wearer beloved by God and man. He passed it on by will to his favourite son, with instructions that he should do likewise. So it passed down many generations until it came to one who had three sons all equally dear to him. Not wishing to favour one more than the others, he had two replicas made, and thus gave each of his sons a ring. After his death each son claimed to possess the true ring, and a quarrel broke out between them. The true ring could not be identified—"almost as for us the true faith is now beyond discovery." A judge brought in to arbitrate decided that none of the three quarrelling brothers could rightly claim to possess it. Presumably the true ring must therefore have been lost, and the father must have had three rings made to replace it. Nevertheless, by love and brotherly conduct each should try to show that his own ring possessed the power of the ancient ring. Only so, if at all, might the identity of the true ring be determined.

The theology of *Nathan* is the familiar eighteenth-century thesis that all the "positive" religions are equally true to those who believe them, equally false to the philosophers, and equally useful to the magistrates: that the only absolute is the universal "natural religion" of humanity as a whole. What is required of man is not adherence to dogma but sincerity, tolerance, and brotherly love. The message of *Nathan* is that of the *Testament of John*.[1]

---

[1] Cf. the Savoyard priest in Rousseau's *Émile* (Everyman ed., p. 272): "This is the unwilling scepticism in which I rest; but this scepticism is in no way painful to me, for it does not extend to matters of practice, and I am well assured as to the principles underlying all my duties. I serve God in the simplicity of my heart; I only seek to know what affects my conduct. As to those dogmas which have no effect upon action and morality, dogmas about which so many men torment themselves, I give no heed to them. I regard all individual religions as so many wholesome institutions which prescribe a uniform method by which each country may do honour to God in public worship. . . . God rejects no homage, however offered, provided it is sincere."

Lessing's idea of the universal brotherhood of man and his indifference to all particular religious systems made him strongly attracted to freemasonry. In 1771 he was initiated at Hamburg. It is evident that he was bitterly disappointed with freemasonry as he found it in experience, but he continued to be attracted by its ideals and by its esotericism. In 1778 he published the first three dialogues of *Ernst und Falk*, two more following in 1780.[1] He has no particular use for the ceremonies of freemasonry. "A Lodge bears the same relationship to freemasonry as a Church does to the faith."[2] The masonic organization will not last for ever. The important thing is a freemasonry of the spirit, transcending not only religious and class distinctions, but racial and national divisions which are the inevitable and evil consequence of organizing mankind in separate states. Lessing would foster an internationalism. It is "very much to be hoped that in every state there may be men who are free of the prejudices of nationality and well aware at what point patriotism ceases to be a virtue."[3]

Lessing had no reservations about subscribing to the deist thesis that basic Christianity is perfectly simple ethical teaching, merely loving one's neighbour. This is the leading motif of his early *Thoughts on the Moravians* of 1750 (first printed in 1784). He pleads for their toleration at a time when they were being attacked, contrasting the simplicity of their religion with the highly theological orthodoxy of their opponents. "How simple and vivid was the religion of Adam? But how long did it last?" The world soon sank into a degraded and conventional religion of priests, sacrifices, and mysteries. "So Christ came. Forgive me that here I may treat him only as a teacher enlightened by God." It was his work to restore simplicity and sincerity, to teach that "God is a spirit who must be worshipped in the spirit." But the old corruption has continued, and now Christian teaching is so mixed up with secular wisdom that "a true Christian is far rarer than in the dark ages; in knowledge we are angels, in conduct we are devils."

This essay shows him thinking as a commonplace deist (though writing with a distinction that is only his). A similar standpoint appears in several of the fragments published after his death by his brother

---

[1] English translation in A. Cohen, *Lessing's Masonic Dialogues* (1927). Discussion in H. Schneider, *Lessing* (Bern, 1951), pp. 166–97.

[2] *Ernst und Falk*, iv.

[3] *Ibid.*, ii.

Karl, as, for example, *The Religion of Christ* and *On the Origin of Revealed Religion*. Nevertheless, these fragments represent questions as much as answers in his mind. There is a deeper gulf between Lessing and the Enlightenment than these fragments might lead us to imagine. To his mind there appeared to be too few possibilities. The orthodox were fools. The liberal theologians of Halle were knaves. The enlightened could be too cleverly superficial. Lessing kept up a close and friendly correspondence with his enlightened friends Nicolai and Mendelssohn. But unknown to them the movement of his mind was carrying him away from them, and he stood with them in hardly more than his negative attitude to orthodoxy and the positive religions. "In fact Lessing stood scarcely closer to his Berlin friends than Socrates to the sophist enlightenment at Athens."[1] A letter he wrote to Herder on 25 January 1780 indicates that he felt himself to be steering a middle course between orthodoxy and radical deism. The points where he begins to diverge are the questions that he begins to ask about history, and in those that he puts to the dominant philosophy of Leibniz and the neglected Spinoza.

[1] E. Hirsch, *Geschichte der neuern evangelischen Theologie*, iv (1952), p. 125.

II. HISTORY AND REVELATION

According to Leibniz's theory of knowledge there are two kinds of truths: necessary truths of reason, and contingent truths, knowledge of which is attained by the senses. "The original proof of necessary truths comes from the understanding alone, and all other truths come from experiences or from observations of the senses."[1] Truths of reason belong to a higher order and valuation than mere truths of fact. For "truths of reason are necessary and their opposite is impossible; those of fact are contingent and their opposite is possible."[2] Truths of fact are thus less certain and more untidy; truths of reason are tidy, mathematically certain, and known *a priori*.

Seventeenth-century philosophy is not at ease with the untidiness and irrationality of history. Spinoza, who beside Leibniz was Lessing's favourite philosophical reading, depreciates the significance of history for supporting theological statements. Natural divine law, he writes,

"does not depend on the truth of any historical narrative whatsoever, for inasmuch as this natural divine law is comprehended solely by the consideration of human nature, it is plain that we can conceive it as existing as well in Adam as in any other man. . . . The truth of a historical narrative, however assured, cannot give us the knowledge nor consequently the love of God, for love of God springs from knowledge of him, and knowledge of him should be derived from general ideas, in themselves certain and known, so that the truth of a historical narrative is very far from being a necessary requisite for our attaining our highest good."[3]

Such language lies behind the arguments of Lessing's famous tract *On the Proof of the Spirit and of Power*. The title is taken from Origen, *Contra Celsum*, i. 2, where Origen cites Paul's words in 1 Cor. ii. 5 as

[1] *New Essays on the Human Understanding*, I, i, 5 (Everyman ed., p. 170; A. G. Langley's ed., p. 81). Cf. Nicolas of Cusa, *de Docta Ignorantia*, iii, 4 (tr. G. Heron, pp. 139–40).
[2] *Monadology*, 33 (Everyman ed., p. 9). For Lessing's debt to Leibniz see R. Zimmermann, *Leibnitz und Lessing*, Sitzungsberichte d. Akad. d. Wiss. zu Wien, xvi (1855), pp. 326–91.
[3] *Tractatus theologico-politicus*, iv (tr. Elwes, p. 61).

as if they referred to the two main props of traditional apologetic, prophecy and miracle. The tract is of great importance for understanding Lessing; yet it may be doubted whether any writing equally influential in the history of modern religious thought has been marked by a comparable quantity of logical ambiguity. His first anxiety is to undermine the unqualified certainty which, according to orthodox apologetic, attaches to prophecy and miracle. Both depend upon historical testimony and are therefore to be accepted on the reliability of that testimony. Unqualified certainty is not available for anyone not there at the time. If all "historical truths" are uncertain, then they cannot prove anything. In short, "accidental truths of history can never become the proof of necessary truths of reason." The resurrection of Christ is a past event; it cannot prove the truth that he is Son of God, an idea "against which my reason rebels." The argument jumps from one category of truths to a completely different category, and "if that is not a μετάβασις εἰς ἄλλο γένος then I do not know what Aristotle meant by this phrase. . . . That is the ugly, broad ditch which I cannot get across, however often and however earnestly I have tried to make the leap."

Lessing's strong style of argumentation tends to obscure the latent obscurity and confusion. The ditch, if not wider, is much deeper than he seems to have perceived. Analysis suggests that various ideas, properly distinguishable from one another, have become fused together for him:

1. All certainty about past events is impossible where knowledge of them is dependent upon testimony, not upon firsthand experience. Knowledge of such events does not attain to more than a degree of probability, high or low in accordance with the worth of the testimony.

2. It would have been easier to believe in Christ if only one could have been a contemporary observer of him.

3. The notion that the man Jesus Christ was and is Son of God, "of one substance with the Father," is contrary to reason.

4. Events cannot prove "truths." Truths of morals and metaphysics belong to a non-event category.

5. The realm of historical experience is one of process and flux, the sphere of becoming, not of being. Everything in this flowing process of history is relative, nothing absolute. God, on the other hand, belongs to the ideal world, and truths of divine revelation are timeless truths.

Some of the confusion was perceived by Coleridge, who inscribed the following comment in his copy, now in the British Museum:

"Year after year I have made a point of reperusing the *Kleine Schriften*, as masterpieces of style and argument. But in the Reasoning from [pp.] 115 to 125 [i.e. the present tract] I feel at each reperusal more and more puzzled how so palpable a *miss* could have been made by so acute a mind. He ought to have denied in the first instance and under all circumstances the possible consequences of a speculative conviction from a supposed miracle, having no connection with the doctrine asserted; ex. gr. a man cut a grindstone in half with his thumb. I saw it with my own eyes. Therefore, there are three and only three self-subsisting Persons in the Unity of the Deity. But L. having conceded this, it is absurd to affirm that the most unquestioned and unquestionable historic evidence (ex. gr. that George the third was not the Son but the Grandson of George the Second, to me who live under George the 4th) is in no degree a substitute for the evidence of my own senses—that the conviction produced by such *best possible* confluences of Testimony bears *no* proportion to the conviction produced in me by the recollection (i.e. testimony of my memory) of my own experience.

"As well—or with only one degree more of paradox—might Lessing have applied the same reasoning to the eye-witness's own *recollection* of the Miracle compared with *the seeing* it. . . ."

Lessing's antithesis between the "accidental truths of history" and the "necessary truths of reason" foreshadows the language of German idealism. For Fichte (deeply influenced by Lessing), "only the metaphysical can save, never the historical." And for Kant before him, "the historical can serve only for illustration, not for demonstration." Lessing is driving a wedge between "event" and "truth" which prepares the way for the divorcing of the Gospel history from the "eternal truths" of Christianity in D. F. Strauss (strikingly anticipated in Schleiermacher's *Christmas Eve*, 1806), and for the high valuation of idea and depreciation of past event which runs through Newman's *Essay on Development*.

The actual arguments are commonplaces, and say little that was not said, perhaps more tediously, by others before him. Locke, for example, observes that "any testimony, the farther off it is from the original truth, the less force and proof it has," a remark necessitated (he thinks) by the human propensity to suppose that "opinions gain force by growing older." This has repercussions for the idea of revelation; for

"our assent can reach no higher than the evidence of its being a revelation. . . . If the evidence of its being a revelation, or that this is its true sense, be only on probable proofs, our assent can reach no higher than an assurance or diffidence, arising from the more or less apparent probability of the proofs" (*Essay Concerning Human Understanding*, iv. 16. 10, 14).

And before Locke the problem is stated in a form rather closer to that of Lessing by Lord Herbert of Cherbury:

"All tradition and history, everything in short that concerns the past, whether it be true or false, good or evil, possesses for us only probability, since it depends on the authority of the narrator. . . . Since what is believed in this way makes no direct impression on the faculties, though it may be true for the writer it will be merely probable for those who receive it at second hand."

History he writes off as theologically irrelevant: "My belief in God . . . is not derived from history, but from the teaching of the Common Notions."[1]

The deist John Toland is more simple and blunt:

"All positive matters of fact, duly attested by coevous persons as known to them, and successively related by others of different times, nations, or interests, who could neither be impos'd upon themselves, nor be justly suspected of combining together to deceive others, ought to be receiv'd by us for as certain and indubitable as if we had seen them with our own eyes, or heard them with our own ears. By this means it is, I believe, there was such a city as Carthage, such a reformer as Luther, and that there is such a kingdom as Poland."[2]

But Matthew Tindal[3] echoes Herbert of Cherbury, and the idea that the claims of the Christian revelation rest upon events of which we

---

[1] *De Veritate*, xi. I cite M. H. Carré's translation (Bristol, 1937). Cf. also Hume's *Treatise of Human Nature*, iii. 13.
[2] *Christianity Not Mysterious*, I, iii. 11 (ed. 1702, p. 17).
[3] *Christianity as Old as the Creation* (1730), pp. 161 ff.

have not more than probable reports becomes part of the stock-in-trade of the deist armoury. Rousseau's Savoyard priest repeats the commonplaces and sums up:

> "See what your so-called supernatural proofs, your miracles, your prophecies come to; believe all this upon the word of another, submit to the authority of men the authority of God which speaks to my reason. If the eternal truths which my mind conceives of could suffer any shock, there would be no sort of certainty for me; and far from being sure that you speak to me on God's behalf, I should not even be sure that there is a God."[1]

In *The Proof of the Spirit and of Power* Lessing denies disbelief in such supernatural events as miracles and fulfilled prophecy. But he certainly shared the general eighteenth-century attitude that the supernatural was not a hypothesis to be readily invoked. The age is "rationalist" precisely in the sense of being anti-supernaturalist. The tradition of Christian apologetic from Justin Martyr onwards had seen in miracle and the fulfilment of Old Testament prophecy the main props of Christian truth. The ancient world was not unaccustomed to the idea of the supernatural, and partly on this account ancient Christian apologetic tended to value the fulfilment of prophecy even higher than the evidence of miracle. Celsus, the pagan critic of Christianity, writing about 177–80 A.D., does not deny that the miracles of Jesus happened. He asserts they were done by magic learnt in his youth on his visit to Egypt. And Origen's significant reply affirms that the uniqueness of Jesus' wonders consists in the fact that they were morally far more beneficial than those of magicians.[2] Neither pagan nor Christian finds difficulty in the idea of events transcending the more normal course of nature. In criticizing the argument from the fulfilment of Old Testament prophecy Celsus does not object to the idea of prediction as such; the ancient world had plenty of oracles, sibyls, seers, and experts in clairvoyance. His argument is directed against the Christian claim that

---

[1] *Émile*, Everyman ed., pp. 265–6. The last point, that to undermine the validity of the eternal truths known by the light of natural reason must lead to universal scepticism, is also made by Tindal, p. 345. This indeed was the effect of Bishop Butler's argument in the *Analogy* that there is no difficulty in revelation not paralleled in nature. The boomerang nature of the argument is manifest in the story of Newman, and was clear to J. S. Mill and Leslie Stephen.

[2] Celsus in Origen, *Contra Celsum*, i. 28, 38; ii. 48 ff.

the prophets, living several hundred years before the time of Jesus, predicted precisely the events of his life. He claims that the prophecies which the Christians applied to Jesus were obscurely worded, and with equal or even more plausibility could refer to thousands of other people.[1]

Traditional apologetic had a third argument, which also had its roots in the ancient church, namely, the miraculous expansion of Christianity in the ancient world. That the church could advance from a small Palestinian sect, led by a few fishermen, to become in a mere three hundred years the religion of the Roman emperor and then of the empire itself could only be explained as the work of God.

About 1763–64 Lessing put together some notes (published after his death by his brother Karl), "Of the Manner and Method of Expansion and Spread of the Christian Religion," in which he examines the ancient evidence. The expansion of Christianity, he concludes, was a purely natural phenomenon, and Christian apologists had exaggerated the efficiency of persecution and the number of the martyrs in order to make the astonishing spread of the faith only explicable on the supernaturalistic view.[2]

These, in short, were the "historical" arguments for the faith which had been discredited by the English deists. To the Enlightenment prophecy and miracle are no longer evidences of the truth of Christianity. Spinoza's treatment of the subject in the *Tractatus theologico-politicus* is typical of what was to follow him. Miracle he treats as a purely philosophical question, and argues its impossibility on metaphysical grounds. Prophecy he admits; but he can do so because he entirely eliminates from it the notion of the prediction of the future, and treats it simply as inspired insight into the meaning of contemporary events. In the Age of Reason if Christianity is accepted it is on account of its ethical teaching. To say Christ is Son of God is to say that he is the incarnation of man's highest aspirations and ideals. The apologist may argue that if God was indeed in Christ miracle and the fulfilment of prophecy may be expected; or he may urge that at least the faith in miracles represents an attitude towards Christ which is

[1] Celsus in Origen, *Contra Celsum*, ii. 28.
[2] Lessing handles the argument briefly in the *Vindication of Cardanus* (Lachmann-Muncker, v, p. 321).

essentially the right one. But miracle and prophecy have ceased to be in themselves evidence pointing to the truth of the faith. Instead of being the apologist's strongest asset, they have become an embarrassing liability.

What underlies this is the growing feeling that the world can be explained from within itself; it is a closed system, and the supernatural is an unnecessary or even dangerous hypothesis. For long centuries Christian apologists had talked as if God were virtually another name for the sum of hitherto undiscovered knowledge; as if religion were merely a matter of "filling in logical gaps with devotional material"; as if it were some consolation to believers that the Fellows of the Royal Society had not yet explained everything, and there was thus still some room left for God in the general scheme of things; as if in miracle and prophecy they could point to events which were incapable of being understood by any reasonable man except as proving the decisive intervention of God in nature and history and so vindicating the truth of the Christian revelation.

Moreover, if they were Protestant apologists they talked as if they had an absolute guarantee of revelation in a completely infallible Bible; as if they had one day been browsing in a library and come across a collection of ancient books bound together in one volume, begun to read it, and found to their astonishment that it had no errors in it whether of faith and morals or of history and science, so that they were forced to the conclusion that the work must have been designed as a unity by a divine mind and written at the dictation of the Holy Ghost. If they were Roman Catholics, they talked as if they had spent several years studying the utterances of the bishops of Rome, discovered that the Popes had never been mistaken, and concluded from this that they must be infallible and therefore by their utterances constituted an external, divinely given guarantee of the truths of Christian dogma. Roman and non-Roman alike tended to present positions affirmed on a priori grounds as if they had been reached by empirical methods. Both were anxious to affirm that the supernatural was necessary, since without this hypothesis the phenomena of breaks in the natural order, observed in the Bible or in church history, could not reasonably be accounted for.

"Because the Supernatural is not manifest to the senses, it had been assumed, both by those who maintained its reality and by those who denied it, that it must be proved from the Natural, which is."[1] Accordingly, for Lessing and the Enlightenment as much as for Goeze and the orthodox, the natural and the supernatural appear in radical antithesis to one another. *The Education of the Human Race* shows Lessing using language which in some degree cuts across the traditional antithesis. He wants to change the terms of reference of the debate. Some of the ideas he takes from the *Essay on the History of Civil Society*, by Adam Ferguson (1766), a German translation of which appeared at Leipzig in 1768; Mendelssohn sent it to Lessing in December 1770.[2] Ferguson criticized Rousseau's idea of the original goodness of uncivilized human nature. He believed that history had brought man out of his wild, barbaric state, and represented an advance, not a retrogression.[3]

The first fifty-three sections of *The Education of the Human Race* were published in 1777 as a counter to the fourth fragment of Reimarus, "That the Books of the Old Testament were Not Written to Reveal a Religion." Lessing explicitly regarded the propositions as telling against the simple view of Reimarus, though the weapons of his refutation are not those of orthodox defenders of the faith. The fundamental idea is that the retrospective look of deism is an error. The conventional picture, exemplified in Rousseau or in the deist fragments of Lessing himself (*Thoughts on the Moravians, On the Origin of Revealed Religion*), conceived of an original, primordial "natural religion" which had been corrupted by priestcraft, and in the course of the historical process had steadily deteriorated in the positive religions. The main propositions of *The Education of the Human Race* stand in strong contrast to this. The primary theme is that the positive religions are not retrograde corruptions, or at best mere popular republications, of the religion of nature, but are rather to be seen as stages in the advance of humanity from infancy to maturity.[4] But Lessing does not achieve any genuine consistency. The deist standpoint is not really abandoned (cf. § 4). And his outlook has not ceased to be retrospective, since he

---

[1] J. Oman, *The Natural and the Supernatural* (1931), p. 51.

[2] Lessing's letter of 9 January 1771.

[3] Leslie Stephen, *English Thought in the Eighteenth Century*, ii, pp. 214–16, observes that Ferguson enjoyed a considerable reputation in his time which his undistinguished writings do little to justify.

[4] E. Cassirer, *The Philosophy of the Enlightenment*, p. 194, interprets *The Education* as Lessing's filling-in of the ditch which he could not cross in *The Proof of the Spirit and of Power*. This is to exaggerate and to overestimate him.

thinks it a commendation of his final speculations concerning the transmigration of souls that this notion belongs to the most ancient religious tradition (§ 95).[1] On top of his primitivist belief in a primordial religion of nature, he merely superimposes the idea of humanity's progress,[2] seen in the advance of the Israelites out of primitive barbarism into an ethical monotheism, with the teaching of Jesus as the culmination of the biblical story.

Lessing particularly commends his view to orthodox defenders of the faith on the ground that it will set the problem of the Old Testament in a new light. From his new point of view deficiencies and moral difficulties in it need not shock us, and certainly constitute no argument against the "truth" of the Bible. If the doctrine of immortality, one of the certainties of Natural Theology, is not taught there, that should not invalidate its claim to attention or its status as part of the story of revelation. The notion of revelation as a process of education rather than as a once-for-all communication of timeless truths eliminates the need for the ingenious subtleties of Bishop William Warburton, who had paradoxically argued that it is precisely the absence of any such teaching in the Old Testament which is the decisive proof of its divine origin.[3] Without a doctrine of retribution after death, Warburton said, morality would dissolve and no state could survive. The Jewish nation succeeded in so doing. God must therefore have provided a miraculous substitute for the doctrine of a future life. By special providence he arranged that every Jew should be rewarded in this life in exact proportion to his merits according to his measure of obedience

---

[1] Cf. also Lessing's posthumously printed fragment "That Man may have more than Five Senses" (Lachmann-Muncker, xvi, p. 525), written *c.* 1780–81 after reading Bonnet's *Palingenesia*, which he read in July 1780: "This system of mine is certainly the oldest of all philosophical systems. For it is really nothing but the system of pre-existence of souls and metempsychosis which was held not only by Pythagoras and Plato but also before them by Egyptians and Chaldæans and Persians, in short, by all wise men of the East. And this must be regarded as a point in its favour. The first and most ancient opinion is in speculative matters always the most probable, because sound human understanding at once deteriorated."

[2] For similar inconsistency in Herder cf. A. O. Lovejoy, *Essays in the History of Ideas* (1948), pp. 166–82.

[3] W. Warburton, *The Divine Legation of Moses* (1738). For an acid account of his extraordinary apologetic see Stephen, *op. cit.*, i, pp. 355 ff. Lessing reviewed the German translation of 1751 in the *Berlinische Privilegirte Zeitung* (Lachmann-Muncker, iv, pp. 373–4), and was evidently impressed (cf. xiv, p. 310).

to the law. Belief in a future life was thus replaced by a succession of supernatural interventions with the natural order.

Warburton's subtlety is self-defeating. The story of the Old Testament is rather to be seen as a progressive revelation—or at any rate as a progressive discovery and advance on the part of man.

This antithesis (discovery or revelation?) appears at its most acute when §§ 4 and 77 are set side by side.[1] Here in one and the same work Lessing is apparently contradicting himself. In § 77 he grants that Christianity, however dubious its historical credentials, has led humanity to insights concerning God and man which would never have been achieved by human reason unaided. Yet in § 4 he insists categorically that "revelation gives nothing to the human race which human reason could not arrive at on its own." Ultimately therefore revelation is superfluous. Its content passes over without break into the insights of reason, and it has therefore lost any connection with the idea of divine transcendence. Its difference from reason is merely quantitative, not qualitative. It is only another name for the upsurging of the human spirit in its development towards maturity.

Lessing is not unaware of the difficulty. Included in the bromide for the laity in his Counter-propositions to Reimarus is the question: "What is a revelation which reveals nothing? Is it enough to preserve the mere name though the thing has already been discarded?"

His solution in § 4 is to suggest that revelation, though ultimately unnecessary inasmuch as reason will get there in the end, is a help in accelerating the advance towards the goal.

Take away the idea of progress in history, and this is all very close to the Savoyard priest:

---

[1] The antithesis between these two sections is the starting-point of a stimulating study of Lessing by H. Thielicke, *Vernunft und Offenbarung* (1936). He explains the tension by interpreting "reason" in two different senses. In § 4 Lessing is using the word in the sense of Kant's *Critique of Pure Reason*. It is not empirical, but transcendental, a power to make analytic and synthetic *a priori* judgments. In § 77 the idea is that the empirical reason can only be elevated to full apprehension by revelation which mediates between the transcendental and the empirical reason. Thielicke's study is of much interest and value, but his main thesis is hard to accept, and I fear I cannot share his conviction that Lessing was quite incapable of contradicting himself in one and the same work; cf. the tension noted above between the idea of progress in history, and his retrospective regard for primordial religious ideas; also that between § 22 and the idea of transmigration in the last sections.

＊"Reason tells me that dogmas should be plain, clear, and striking in their simplicity. If there is something lacking in natural religion, it is with respect to the obscurity in which it leaves the great truths it teaches; revelation should teach us these truths in a way which the mind of man can understand; it should bring them within his reach, make him comprehend them, so that he may believe them."[1]

This new approach does not merely ease some of the difficulties of the Old Testament. It also sets miracles in a fresh light. They may now be seen as the swaddling-clothes of the infant church. The belief in the miraculous stands in its place as a stage in the emergent evolution of the human religious consciousness. To discard the Gospels, to become angry with them because they contain miracle-stories, is to adopt an essentially unhistorical point of view, and we have no right to demand that the men of the first century should share the world-view of the eighteenth. This belief is an element in Lessing's hostility towards the liberalizing theology of Semler and his school; he scorns those who want to preserve the New Testament while reducing its miraculous content. Nothing provoked more wrath in him than the reply to Reimarus made by Semler himself.[2]

It has not perhaps been sufficiently recognized how much the ideas of *The Education of the Human Race* go back to Lessing's reading of the early Church Fathers, especially the Christian Platonists of Alexandria, Clement and Origen. In Origen's thought redemption is achieved by a long, slow process of divine education. In the Bible the divine revelation is accommodated to the form suited to every capacity, expressed in

---

[1] Rousseau, *Émile*, Everyman ed., p. 264.

[2] J. S. Semler, *Beantwortung der Fragmente eines Ungenannten*, 1779 (I have only seen the second, revised edition of 1780). This long and undoubtedly very able reply is directed against Reimarus, not against Lessing. Most of the criticisms are concerned with the deficiencies of Reimarus' scholarly equipment, and it must be admitted that in this respect Reimarus delivered himself into his critic's hands at too many points. Semler rightly insists that almost all his objections are valid only if Christianity is committed to belief in an inerrant Bible (2nd ed., p. 267), and that Reimarus' misleading account of Christian origins justifies him in making this reply which is not, as some supposed, inconsistent with his own demands for free historical inquiry. Reimarus' treatment of the resurrection is vitiated by his idea that it is to be handled as a past event on the same plane as any other event in the natural order, which evacuates it of religious significance. "It is not a merely physical event . . . it is supernatural" (p. 261). For discussion see L. Zscharnack, *Lessing und Semler* (1905).

straightforward terms for the simple, in terms of mystery for the instructed believer. If we find God in the Old Testament using threats and appearing as a wrathful and vengeful deity, that is no argument against the belief that divine revelation is contained therein, as had been urged by the second-century heretic Marcion. Admittedly such language does not at all correspond to God's true nature. But it is used on account of human frailty, just as human fathers sometimes appear other than they really are in order to discipline their children. The purpose of all divine punishment is beneficial and remedial. It is part of the process of the education of humanity. The believer begins by accepting the faith on trust. But as his education advances he learns the reasons underlying the beliefs which he first accepted on authority, and tests them by rational argument. God gradually teaches him, if he will, to learn more of his true being, first in this life, and then hereafter where the process of higher education will be continued. Biblical language about the pains of hell really refers to the purifying, divine fire which purges away the dross from human souls. And heaven is a place of gradation through which the saints pass as they learn more and more of the divine love.

to some extent true

disagrees

The similarity between all this and the essay *Leibniz on Eternal Punishments* is at once apparent. In *The Education of the Human Race* (85 ff.) the speculations about "the eternal gospel" are connected with the anticipations in Joachim and the spiritual Franciscans. He was perhaps as much influenced by Origen's comparable ideas.[1] And he may also have found in Origen some justification for his notions of the pre-existence and the transmigration of souls.

Perhaps, however, the most important idea that Lessing seems to have derived from his reading in the Alexandrians is his insistence that absolute certainties are not accessible to frail human beings in their present life in which they can only see through a glass, darkly. His

[1] Cf. C. Bigg, *The Christian Platonists of Alexandria*, 1913, pp. 269 ff. Origen's doctrine of the Eternal Gospel is discussed by Leibniz in the *Theodicy*, i. 17–18 (ed. Farrer, pp. 132 f.). The idea of the uncertainty of all historical knowledge is also present in Origen (*Contra Celsum*, i. 42), but it is not from this source that Lessing derives the argument which is a commonplace of the age. Origen's depreciation of the value of the historical can be exaggerated (cf. R. L. P. Milburn, *Early Christian Interpretations of History*, 1954, pp. 38–53); but a certain devaluation of the process of history is a perennial characteristic of all idealism, whether in Plato, Clement and Origen, Leibniz and Lessing, Bernard Bosanquet and W. R. Inge.

difficulty with orthodoxy is the confidence of its dogma, the un-mitigated, unqualified assertiveness of its claims to know the answers. A little more hesitancy and diffidence would be to him a better com-mendation of its claims to communicate revelation. "Revealed religion, we are told, alone gives us complete and indubitable certainty of the immortality of the soul. Reason provides us with mere probabilities in this matter." Lessing objects not only that this is untrue for the reason that the credentials of the Christian revelation rest upon mere historical probabilities and not upon certainties, but, furthermore, that even if it were true, this certainty would in itself constitute an argument against Christianity. Against astrology it is argued that it is not expedient for man to know the future exactly.

"This ground for rejecting astrology is a ground for rejecting all revealed religion. For even if it were true that there is an art of knowing the future, we would rather not learn it. And even if it were true that there is a religion which gives us absolutely certain teaching concerning the future life, yet we would choose not to listen to this religion for one moment."

The higher the claims of revealed religion, the less plausible they are.[1]

Lessing's individualism asserts against the confident pronouncements of revealed theology the need for a continual search for truth. Absolute truth is not revealed; but if it were our minds would not wish, even if, being finite, they are nevertheless able, to apprehend it. Clement of Alexandria had affirmed that the perfect or "gnostic" Christian searches for the knowledge of God without any selfish desire for the personal possession of salvation; for it is essential to the rational being that he should eternally exercise his reason. If, he adds, we could put before the "gnostic" the choice between knowledge of God and everlasting salva-tion, he would unhesitatingly choose the knowledge of God.[2] In his *Rejoinder* of 1778 Lessing adapts these words to form the most famous of all his sayings:

"The worth of a man does not consist in the truth he possesses, or thinks he possesses, but in the pains he has taken to attain that truth.

[1] *Womit sich die geoffenbarte Religion am meisten weiss, macht mir sie gerade am verdächtigsten* (Lachmann-Muncker, xvi, pp. 399–400), first printed by Karl Lessing in 1795, probably written *c.* 1777–78.
[2] *Stromateis*, iv. 136.

For his powers are extended not through possession but through the search for truth. In this alone his ever-growing perfection consists. Possession makes him lazy, indolent, and proud.

"If God held all truth in his right hand and in his left the everlasting striving after truth, so that I should always and everlastingly be mistaken, and said to me, 'Choose,' with humility I would pick on the left hand and say, 'Father, grant me that. Absolute truth is for thee alone.'"[1]

For the restless mind of Lessing there cannot be answers in the sense that there were both for the orthodox and for the Enlightenment, where knowledge was conceived of in a static fashion as a possession to be enjoyed in contentment. For him it is an everlasting inquiry to be ceaselessly pursued, a never-ending quest.

It follows that the elucidation of his "system" is subject to particular difficulties. The target to be hit by the student of his writings is never still, but is rapidly moving. Moreover, the manner in which he conducts his theological campaign makes it absurd to construct his system merely by gathering together his many diverse utterances. The arguments are so often presented *ad hominem*. He is all things to all men. To his Berlin friends he adopts the conventions of the Enlightenment. To church people he uses Christian language.

The Education of the Human Race looks at first sight uncommonly like an acceptance, in admittedly modified terms, of the Christian revelation. In the nineteenth century many readers of Lessing undoubtedly so understood him, and clearly this interpretation was intended by Lessing himself. But it is uncertain whether even here Lessing has disclosed himself entirely, and whether he really believed in any *transcendent* revelation whatever.

In a fundamental study of Lessing's attitude to Christianity Friedrich Loofs argued that all his language accepting the idea of revelation was merely exoteric and designed for public consumption, whereas he concealed his true opinions so thoroughly that it is now futile to try and discover them.[2] His letters to his brother and to Elise Reimarus at the time of the controversy with Goeze indicate beyond doubt that the

[1] *Eine Duplik*, Lachmann-Muncker, xiii, pp. 23–4.
[2] "Lessings Stellung zum Christentum," in *Theologische Studien und Kritiken*, 83 (1913), pp. 31–64.

Counter-propositions to Reimarus were intended as bromide, and do not represent his real opinions. Loofs concludes that the "Christian" reading of *The Education of the Human Race* is equally dubious. This too is in some degree exoteric. The enlightened thought it morally justifiable to conceal their true opinions behind the mask of orthodoxy. John Toland had made a special study of the practices of ancient philosophers in teaching one thing to the crowd and another to the inner circle of chosen disciples.[1] In *The Education of the Human Race* (68 f.) Lessing points clearly in this direction (and he writes similarly in *Leibniz on Eternal Punishments*). It is not unlikely that behind the semi-orthodox language he conceals a radicalism even deeper than that of his Berlin friends.

All Lessing's theological writings, whether cast in dialogue form or not (and it is no accident that this form was congenial to him), are an intellectual debate with exchange of question and answer. The difficulty is to know precisely what is question and what is answer. Loofs interprets him as a man with radical answers (the precise nature of which is beyond discovery), who for the sake of argument and debate asks some theistic-sounding questions. Thielicke (cf. above p. 39 n. 1) treats him as at heart a man with more or less theistic answers whose fragmentary notes, published after his death by his brother, show him asking deist questions.

In considering this problem of discovering Lessing's answers one negative point is beyond dispute. He clearly denied the exclusiveness of the traditional idea of special revelation. "Truth" for him does not consist in dogma, except for the dogma that there is no dogma. "Truth" is brotherly love, sincerity, and tolerance rather than a metaphysical interpretation of nature, man, and God. His certainties are moral certainties. Among his papers relating to *Nathan the Wise* there occurs the note: "Nathan's attitude to all positive religions has long been mine."[2] The thesis of *Nathan*, *The Testament of John*, and the masonic dialogues *Ernst und Falk* is unambiguous. Although it cannot be checked, the story is not improbable that when he was told the story of Voltaire receiving on his sickbed the ministrations of the priest of Saint Sulpice he commented: "When you see me dying call for the

---

[1] Toland, "Clidophorus, or of the Exoteric and Esoteric Philosophy," *Tetradymus* (1720), pp. 61–100.

[2] Lachmann-Muncker, xvi, p. 444.

notary; I will declare to him that I die in none of the positive religions."[1]

In assessing the originality of his contribution to thought it is important not to overestimate him. His criticisms of orthodoxy are not new; in all this he belongs to the second or third generation, and his originality in ideas is not great. In a moment of self-examination and reflection he wrote: "I am not a scholar, I have never intended to become a scholar; I could not be a scholar even if it were possible in a dream. All that I have made some small attempt to achieve is the ability to use a learned book in case of necessity."[2] What is wholly original in Lessing is not the argument but the fire and force of its expression, the provocative, sharply formulated sentences, the constant irony, the parry and thrust of debate. He compels the reader to pursue the quarry with him so that he feels himself personally involved. His enormous influence upon the European mind is in no small measure to be attributed to this wonderful command of language and to the wide range of his cultured, humanistic interest in art and classical literature.

If a system is a tidy set of neat and coherent answers, Lessing has no system. Undoubtedly he would have rejected even the possibility of such answers. His propositions are questions even where they are cast in the grammatical form of statements. Nevertheless it is not necessary wholly to abandon the search for his world-view. Certain indications make it fairly clear which way his mind was moving.

The theologians of the Enlightenment did not reject the Bible; they found in it only natural religion. Although they made no special appeal to miracle and prophecy, they accepted the supernaturalist hypothesis in the sense that they repeated traditional language about the transcendence of God. But the rationalism of Leibniz *qua* philosopher rather than *qua* theologian, for all his intentions of remaining a loyal Lutheran, really left little place for divine transcendence. Lessing saw that in the scheme of nature that had come to dominate the mind of the age, this transcendent God, who made no special revelations and was only known to all men alike through the book of nature, was no longer necessary. He may have been the first cause of the world, but

---

1 Cited by Loofs, *loc. cit.*, p. 41.
2 Lachmann-Muncker, xvi, p. 535.

he had not intervened since the beginning.[1] He might as well be dead. In the privacy of his own mind Lessing took the decisive step of eliminating this idea of God being remote and beyond the world, never disclosing himself; there was nothing for him to do. The God of Lessing's personal religion is immanent in nature and history. His operation is to be discerned in the forward-moving impulse of the historical process. He is destiny.[2]

Throughout his life Lessing's mind was in debate with Spinoza. From the *Dictionary* of Pierre Bayle the Enlightenment had received a very hostile picture of him, with the consequence that although he died in 1677 it was more than a century before he came into his own. Lessing read him during his Breslau period, and disputed about the relation between his philosophy and that of Leibniz with his friend Mendelssohn. The fragment *On the Reality of Things outside God* (c. 1763) shows him raising questions concerning the transcendence of God in terms reminiscent of Spinoza, though his language does not at this stage imply any acceptance of Spinoza's system.

In 1785 F. H. Jacobi published his *Letters to Moses Mendelssohn on the Subject of Spinoza's Doctrine*, in which he claimed that in July 1780, not long before Lessing's death (15 February 1781), he visited him at Wolfenbüttel and conversed with him concerning the philosophy of Spinoza. On producing Goethe's poem *Prometheus* he was startled to receive from Lessing the reply that its standpoint contained no shocks for him; he had already accepted all that from Spinoza. "The orthodox ideas of Deity are no longer possible for me; I cannot enjoy them. Ἐν καὶ πᾶν. I know nothing else. . . . There is no other philosophy except the philosophy of Spinoza." Lessing surprised him further by confessing that he was not afraid of the ethical determinism of Spinoza: "I have no desire for free will."

Jacobi's deduction that Lessing was a wholehearted follower of Spinoza horrified the Enlightenment. Mendelssohn was moved to write a counterblast, to vindicate his good name from the scandalous libel contained in Jacobi's revelations, and a furious controversy ensued.[3]

---

[1] Discussing the communication between soul and body in the preface to the *Theodicy* (p. 66, ed. Farrer) Leibniz characteristically comments: "I admit the supernatural here only in the beginning of things."

[2] Cf. F. J. Schneider, *Lessing und die monistische Weltanschauung* (Halle, 1929).

[3] Kant's contribution to the controversy has recently appeared in an English translation by L. W. Beck: *Kant's "Critique of Practical Reason" and Other Writings*

There is no need to doubt the reasonable accuracy of Jacobi's report of Lessing's words. They do not necessitate the conclusion that he had made the whole of Spinoza's system his own, or justify Jacobi's attempt to read Spinoza into *The Education of the Human Race*. The significance of the conversation is the explicit disclosure that Lessing had abandoned any idea of the transcendence of God. His creed is an immanent destiny.

Lessing's denial of free will in the dialogue with Jacobi is coherent with his comments appended to the *Philosophical Articles* of K. W. Jerusalem which he published in 1776 in protest against Goethe's *Werther*. To the third essay, "On Freedom," he notes:

"The third paper shows how well the author grasped a system which is denounced for its dangerous consequences, and would certainly be much more widely accepted if only people could readily become accustomed to regard these consequences in the light in which they here appear. Virtue and vice explained in this way; reward and punishment limited to this: what do we lose if we are denied freedom? Something (if it is anything at all) which we do not need; which we do not need either for our activity here or for our salvation hereafter. Something the possession of which must make us far more disturbed and anxious than the feeling of its opposite can ever make us. Compulsion and necessity, in accordance with which the idea produces the best effect, are much more welcome to me than a bleak power of being able under similar circumstances to act sometimes in one way, sometimes in another. I thank the Creator that I am under necessity; that the best must be. If even within these limitations I still make so many slips, what would happen if I were left entirely to myself? left to a blind force which operates according to no law, and does not less subject me to chance because this chance plays its game within me? From the standpoint of morality, therefore, this system is safe. But cannot speculation raise against it quite different objections? And such objections as can be answered only by a second system equally foreign to the common outlook? It was this which often prolonged our discussion and cannot be briefly set forth here."

in Moral Philosophy (Chicago, 1949), pp. 293–305. The chief documents are collected by H. Scholz, *Die Hauptschriften zum Pantheismusstreit zwischen Jacobi und Mendelssohn* (Berlin, 1916).

The Jacobi-conversation does not mean that Lessing wholly forsook Leibniz. The heritage of Leibniz remains with him, and from this source he derived his deterministic optimism, his belief that all is governed by a beneficent providence to produce the best of all possible worlds in which the best must be, and what must be is best. From Leibniz he takes his idea of a divinely ordered unfolding and development. His philosophical world-view takes over that of Leibniz, *minus* the transcendence of God. It is this crucial divergence which aligns him with Spinoza at the last.

Lessing's personal creed is one thing; his legacy is another. His beliefs present a not unfamiliar phenomenon in religious history. In every age there appear those who write off traditional and institutional forms of religion as formal and conventional, and seek to find an esoteric, basic creed common to all the world-religions, transcending all the customary barriers of race and culture. Usually this basic faith is supposed to have been handed down in secret from time immemorial. Lessing's interest in freemasonry,[1] his speculations concerning the transmigration of souls, and the gnosticism of some of his essays, such as *Leibniz on Eternal Punishments* and *The Christianity of Reason*, are symptomatic.

To give an adequate account of his historical influence would extend this introduction to inordinate lengths. The questions that he asked have dominated, perhaps even haunted, modern theology. His pervasive influence is seen in writers who never read a line of his writings, as well as in Sören Kierkegaard and Coleridge. He plays a prominent part in launching upon nineteenth-century theology the idea of progressive revelation.[2] His indirect influence even upon a man ignorant of German like John Henry Newman is apparent in the wedge he drives between idea and fact, between event and "truth," and in the impetus he gives to the notion (implicit in Newman's *Essay on Development*) of historical inevitability, that whatever is, must be.[3] His

[1] Cf. H. Schneider, *Quest for Mysteries: the Masonic Background for Literature in Eighteenth-Century Germany*, 1947.

[2] His ideas run through *Essays and Reviews* (1860). The first essay by Frederick Temple, "The Education of the World," was no doubt inspired by reading F. W. Robertson's translation of *The Education of the Human Race* (1858). Benjamin Jowett's essay "On the Interpretation of Scripture" is summed up in his maxim: "Interpret the Bible like any other book."

[3] For critical analysis of the idea see I. Berlin, *Historical Inevitability* (1954); G. Ryle, *Dilemmas* (1954), pp. 15-35.

questions concerning the natural and the supernatural are taken up by Schleiermacher, concerning the relation of faith and freedom by Ritschl. His individualism and assertion of the right of private judgment have contributed towards creating the feeling in the minds of many contemporary agnostics that if they are to become Christians they must make so great an intellectual surrender that such a submission can only be reasonably made before the claims to overwhelming supernatural authority of the bishop of Rome. In the immense seriousness of his protest against the conspiracy of silence concerning biblical criticism he is the precursor of the evangelical fervour of Thomas Henry Huxley, making his famous rejoinder to Wilberforce at Oxford in 1860. His questions regarding the uncertainty of historical knowledge remain, and underlie much of the recent controversy concerning the uniting of radical historical scepticism with a profoundly Christian existentialism by Rudolf Bultmann.[1]

[1] The problem appears in a slightly different dress in contemporary Roman Catholic apologetic. Where it may be reasonably argued that the evidence for the resurrection of Christ is sufficient to render the event historically probable, the Roman Catholic is anxious to urge that, by reason of the supernatural *magisterium* of the Church which teaches it as a revealed truth, it is absolutely certain. Reviewing Dr. Austin Farrer's essay in the volume *Kerygma and Myth* (1953), ed. H. W. Bartsch, tr. R. H. Fuller, Dom B. C. Butler remarks: "As a historian I am indeed 'inclined to believe' that Christ was virginally conceived and rose corporeally from the dead. . . . But as a Christian I 'believe' these mysteries on the authority of the *kerygma* of the Church, and therefore with a certainty that historical investigation can never give me. So far as I can see, supernatural faith in the articles of the creed implies the absolute authority of the word of Christ upon the lips of the contemporary Church." (*Downside Review*, lxxii (1954), p. 94.) Dr. Farrer's view he stigmatizes as "pure Gore." But his own standpoint approximates very nearly to that adopted by Gore in the Anglican debates of 1913–14, and in *The New Theology and the Old Religion* (1907), pp. 109 ff.

I

ON THE PROOF OF THE SPIRIT AND OF POWER[1]

... διὰ τὰς τεραστίους δυνάμεις ἃς κατασκευαστέον
γεγονέναι καὶ ἐκ πολλῶν μὲν ἄλλων καὶ ἐκ τοῦ ἴχνη
δὲ αὐτῶν ἔτι σῴζεσθαι παρὰ τοῖς κατὰ τὸ βούλημα
τοῦ λόγου βιοῦσι.[2]

Ὠριγένης κ. Κ.

TO HERR DIRECTOR SCHUMANN AT HANNOVER,

BRUNSWICK, 1777

Sir, who could be more eager to read your new work than I? I hunger for conviction so much that like Erisichthon I swallow everything that has even the appearance of nourishment. If you do the same with this pamphlet, we are the men for one another. I am, with the regard that one inquirer after truth never ceases to bear for another,

Yours etc. ——

Fulfilled prophecies, which I myself experience, are one thing; fulfilled prophecies, of which I know only from history that others say they have experienced them, are another.

Miracles, which I see with my own eyes, and which I have the opportunity to verify for myself, are one thing; miracles, of which I know only from history that others say they have seen them and verified them, are another.

That surely, is beyond controversy? Surely there is no objection to be made against that?

If I had lived at the time of Christ, then of course the prophecies fulfilled in his person would have made me pay great attention to him.

---

[1] *Lessings Werke*, ed. Lachmann-Muncker, xiii, pp. 1–8.
[2] "... because of the prodigious miracles which may be proved to have happened by this argument among many others, that traces of them still remain among those who live according to the will of the Logos" (Origen, *Contra Celsum*, i. 2).

51

If I had actually seen him do miracles; if I had had no cause to doubt that these were true miracles; then in a worker of miracles who had been marked out so long before, I would have gained so much confidence that I would willingly have submitted my intellect to his, and I would have believed him in all things in which equally indisputable experiences did not tell against him.

Or: if I even now experienced that prophecies referring to Christ or the Christian religion, of whose priority in time I have long been certain, were fulfilled in a manner admitting no dispute; if even now miracles were done by believing Christians which I had to recognize as true miracles: what could prevent me from accepting this proof of the spirit and of power, as the apostle calls it?

In the last instance Origen was quite right in saying that in this proof of the spirit and of power the Christian religion was able to provide a proof of its own more divine than all Greek dialectic. For in his time there was still "the power to do miraculous things which still continued" among those who lived after Christ's precept; and if he had undoubted examples of this, then if he was not to deny his own senses he had of necessity to recognize that proof of the spirit and of power.

But I am no longer in Origen's position; I live in the eighteenth century, in which miracles no longer happen. If I even now hesitate to believe anything on the proof of the spirit and of power, which I can believe on other arguments more appropriate to my age: what is the problem?

The problem is that this proof of the spirit and of power no longer has any spirit or power, but has sunk to the level of human testimonies of spirit and power.

The problem is that reports of fulfilled prophecies are not fulfilled prophecies; that reports of miracles are not miracles. These, the prophecies fulfilled before my eyes, the miracles that occur before my eyes, are immediate in their effect. But those—the reports of fulfilled prophecies and miracles, have to work through a medium which takes away all their force.

To quote Origen and to cite his words that "the proof of power is so called because of the astonishing miracles which have happened to confirm the teaching of Christ" is of little use if one keeps from one's readers what Origen says immediately thereafter. For the readers will also turn up Origen and find with surprise that he argues for the truth of the miracles which happened with the foundation of Christianity ἐκ πολλῶν μὲν ἄλλων, thus, from the narrative of the evangelists; chiefly and particularly, however, he argues their truth on the basis of miracles which were still happening.

If then this proof of the proof has now entirely lapsed; if then all historical certainty is much too weak to replace this apparent proof of the proof which has lapsed: how is it to be expected of me that the same inconceivable truths which sixteen to eighteen hundred years ago people believed on the strongest inducement, should be believed by me to be equally valid on an infinitely lesser inducement?

Or is it invariably the case, that what I read in reputable historians is just as certain for me as what I myself experience?

I do not know that anyone has ever asserted this. What is asserted is only that the reports which we have of these prophecies and miracles are as reliable as historical truths ever can be. And then it is added that historical truths cannot be demonstrated: nevertheless we must believe them as firmly as truths that have been demonstrated.

To this I answer: *First*, who will deny (not I) that the reports of these miracles and prophecies are as reliable as historical truths ever can be? But if they are only as reliable as this, why are they treated as if they were infinitely more reliable?

And in what way? In this way, that something quite different and much greater is founded upon them than it is legitimate to found upon truths historically proved.

If no historical truth can be demonstrated, then nothing can be demonstrated by means of historical truths.

That is: *accidental truths of history can never become the proof of necessary truths of reason.*

I do not for one moment deny that in Christ prophecies were fulfilled; I do not for one moment deny that Christ performed miracles. But since the truth of these miracles has completely ceased to be demonstrable by miracles still happening at the present time, since they are no more than reports of miracles (however incontroverted and incontrovertible they may be), I deny that they can and should bind me in the least to a faith in the other teachings of Christ. These other teachings I accept on other grounds.

Then *secondly*: What does it mean to accept an historical proposition as true? to believe an historical truth? Does it mean anything other than this: to accept this proposition, this truth as valid? to accept that there is no objection to be brought against it? to accept that one historical proposition is built on one thing, another on another, that from one historical truth another follows? to reserve to oneself the right to estimate other historical things accordingly? Does it mean anything other than this? Anything more? Examine carefully.

We all believe that an Alexander lived who in a short time conquered almost all Asia. But who, on the basis of this belief, would risk anything of great, permanent worth, the loss of which would be irreparable? Who, in consequence of this belief, would forswear for ever all knowledge that conflicted with this belief? Certainly not I. Now I have no objection to raise against Alexander and his victory: but it might still be possible that the story was founded on a mere poem of Chœrilus just as the ten-year siege of Troy depends on no better authority than Homer's poetry.

If on historical grounds I have no objection to the statement that Christ raised to life a dead man; must I therefore accept it as true that God has a Son who is of the same essence as himself? What is the connection between my inability to raise any significant objection to the evidence of the former and my obligation to believe something against which my reason rebels?

If on historical grounds I have no objection to the statement that this Christ himself rose from the dead, must I therefore accept it as true that this risen Christ was the Son of God?

That the Christ, against whose resurrection I can raise no important historical objection, therefore declared himself to be the Son of God; that his disciples therefore believed him to be such; this I gladly believe from my heart. For these truths, as truths of one and the same class, follow quite naturally on one another.

But to jump with that historical truth to a quite different class of truths, and to demand of me that I should form all my metaphysical and moral ideas accordingly; to expect me to alter all my fundamental ideas of the nature of the Godhead because I cannot set any credible testimony against the resurrection of Christ: if that is not a μετάβασις εἰς ἄλλο γένος, then I do not know what Aristotle meant by this phrase.

It is said: "The Christ of whom on historical grounds you must allow that he raised the dead, that he himself rose from the dead, said himself that God had a Son of the same essence as himself and that he is this Son." This would be quite excellent! if only it were not the case that it is not more than historically certain that Christ said this.

If you press me still further and say: "Oh yes! this is more than historically certain. For it is asserted by inspired historians who cannot make a mistake."

But, unfortunately, that also is only historically certain, that these historians were inspired and could not err.

That, then, is the ugly, broad ditch which I cannot get across, however often and however earnestly I have tried to make the leap. If anyone can help me over it, let him do it, I beg him, I adjure him. He will deserve a divine reward from me.

And so I repeat what I have said above in the same words. I do not for one moment deny that in Christ prophecies were fulfilled. I do not for one moment deny that Christ did miracles. But since the truth of these miracles has completely ceased to be demonstrable by miracles still happening now, since they are no more than reports of miracles (even though they be narratives which have not been, and cannot be, impugned), I deny that they can and should bind me to the very least faith in the other teachings of Christ.

What then does bind me? Nothing but these teachings themselves. Eighteen hundred years ago they were so new, so alien, so foreign to the entire mass of truths recognized in that age, that nothing less than miracles and fulfilled prophecies were required if the multitude were to attend to them at all.

But to make the multitude attentive to something means to put common sense on to the right track.

And so it came about, so it now is. And what it hunted out to the left and right of this track are the fruits of those miracles and fulfilled prophecies.

These fruits I may see before me ripe and ripened, and may I not be satisfied with that? The old pious legend that the hand which scatters the seed must wash in snails' blood seven times for each throw, I do not doubt, but merely ignore it. What does it matter to me whether the legend is false or true? The fruits are excellent.

Suppose that a very useful mathematical truth had been reached by the discoverer through an obvious fallacy. (Even if such an instance does not exist, yet it could exist). Should I deny this truth? Should I refuse to use this truth? Would I be on that account an ungrateful reviler of the discoverer, if I were unwilling to prove from his insight in other respects, indeed did not consider it capable of proof, that the fallacy through which he stumbled upon the truth *could* not be a fallacy?

I conclude, and my wish is: May all who are divided by the Gospel of John be reunited by the Testament of John. Admittedly it is apocryphal, this testament. But it is not on that account any the less divine.

II

THE TESTAMENT OF JOHN

"... qui in pectus Domini recubuit et de purissimo fonte hausit rivulum doctrinarum."

JEROME

HE: You were very quick with this pamphlet [*On the Proof of the Spirit and of Power*]; but the pamphlet shows it.

I: Really?

HE: You usually write more clearly.

I: The greatest clarity I have always regarded as the greatest beauty.

HE: But I see you let yourself be carried away. You begin to think that you can just make allusions to things which are not understood by one in a hundred readers; which perhaps you yourself learnt about only yesterday or the day before. . . .

I: For example?

HE: Don't be too learned.

I: For example?

HE: Your obscure remark at the end. Your Testament of John. I have searched in vain through the pages of my Grabius and Fabricius[1] for it.

I: Must everything be a book, then?

HE: Is this Testament of John not a book? What is it, then?

I: The last will of John, the last remarkable words of the dying John which he repeated over and over again. Cannot they also be called a Testament?

HE: Certainly they can. But I am now less curious about it. Nevertheless, what are these words? I am not very well read in the Abdias,[2] or wherever else they may occur.

I: They are to be found in a less suspect writer. Jerome preserved

---

[1] J. E. Grabius, *Spicilegium SS. Patrum ut et Hæreticorum seculi post Christum natum, I, II, et III* (Oxford, 1714); J. A. Fabricius, *Codex Apocryphus Novi Testamenti* (Hamburg, 1719).

[2] Abdias, Bishop of Babylon, was the alleged author of an apocryphal history of the apostles in ten books; for the Latin text cf. Fabricius, *op. cit.*; English summary in M. R. James, *The Apocryphal New Testament*, pp. 462 ff.

them for us in his *Commentary on Paul's Epistle to the Galatians.* Turn them up there. I hardly think that you will like them.

HE: Who knows? Just quote them to me.

I: Out of my head? Giving the circumstances which I can now remember or which seem to be probable?

HE: Why not?

I: For John, the good John who wished never again to be separated from his Church which he had gathered together at Ephesus, this single congregation was a sufficiently large stage for his teaching of wonders and his wonderful teaching. John was an old man, so old that . . .

HE: That the pious and simple folk thought he would never die.

I: Yet they saw him day by day approaching nearer to death.

HE: Superstition sometimes trusts the senses too much, sometimes too little. Even when John was already dead, superstition still held on to the belief that John *could* not die, that he slept and was not dead.

I: How close superstition often gets to the truth.

HE: But tell me more of the story. I cannot listen to you speaking in favour of superstition.

I: With a speed as hesitant as a friend wrenching himself from the arm of a friend to hasten to the embrace of his lady, gradually and visibly John's pure soul was separated from his equally pure but decayed body. Soon his disciples could not even carry him to church. And yet John would not neglect any assembly; he would allow no assembly to disperse without his address to the community which would rather have been deprived of its daily bread than of this address.

HE: Which often may not have been very carefully prepared.

I: Do you prefer what has been carefully prepared?

HE: It all depends.

I: Is it quite certain that John's address was never that. For it always came straight from his heart. It was always simple and short; and every day became simpler and shorter, until finally he reduced it to the words . . .

HE: To what?

I: "Little children, love one another."

HE: Short and good.

I: Do you really think so? But one so quickly becomes tired of the good and even of the best, if it begins to be an everyday thing. At the first assembly at which John could say no more than "Little children, love one another," these words had a wonderful effect. So it was also in the second, third, and fourth assemblies; for the people said, the weak old man cannot say anything more. But when the old man now and then had good and cheerful days again, and still said nothing more, and still had nothing further for the daily assembly than "Little children, love one another"; when they saw that it was not that the old man was only able to say these few words but that he deliberately chose not to say more: then "Little children, love one another" became insipid, flat, and meaningless. Brethren and disciples could hardly listen any more without feeling sick of it, and finally had the audacity to ask the good old man: "But, Master, why do you always say the same thing?"

HE: And John?

I: John replied: "Because it is the Lord's command; because this alone, this alone, if it is done, is enough, is sufficient and adequate."

HE: So that is your Testament of John?

I: Yes.

HE: It is well that you have called it apocryphal.

I: In contrast to the canonical Gospel of John. But still I think it divine.

HE: In the same sort of way that you would perhaps call a pretty girl divine.

I: I have never called a pretty girl divine, and am not in the habit of misusing this word. What I here call divine Jerome calls *dignam Ioanne sententiam*.

HE: Ah, Jerome!

I: Augustine relates[1] that a certain Platonist said that the beginning of John's Gospel, "In the beginning was the Word," etc., deserves to be inscribed in letters of gold in all churches in the most prominent places.

HE: Of course. The Platonist was quite right. Oh, the Platonists! Quite certainly Plato himself could not have written anything more sublime than these opening words of John's Gospel.

I: That may be. At the same time I, who do not make much of the sublime writing of a philosopher, think that it would be far more appropriate if what was inscribed in letters of gold in all our churches in the most prominent places was the Testament of John.

[1] *City of God*, x. 29.

HE: Hm!

I: "Little children, love one another."

HE: Yes, yes.

I: It was by this Testament of John that formerly one who was of the salt of the earth used to swear. Now he swears by the Gospel of John, and it is said that since this change the salt has become a little stale.

HE: Another riddle?

I: He that has ears to hear let him hear.

HE: Yes, yes, now I see your point.

I: What do you see?

HE: That is how some people always draw their head out of the noose: It is enough if they keep to Christian love; it does not matter what becomes of the Christian religion.

I: Do you count me as one of these people?

HE: Whether I would be right in doing so, you must ask yourself.

I: Then may I say a word for these people?

HE: If you want to do so.

I: But perhaps I do not understand you either. Is then Christian love not the Christian religion?

HE: Yes and no.

I: In what way no?

HE: For the dogmas of the Christian religion are one thing, practical Christianity, which it affirms to be founded upon these dogmas, is another.

I: And in what way yes?

HE: Inasmuch as only that is true Christian love which is founded upon the Christian dogmas.

I: But which of the two is the more difficult? To accept and confess the Christian dogmas, or to practise Christian love?

HE: It would not help you even if I admitted that the latter is by far the more difficult.

I: How then should it help me?

HE: It is all the more ridiculous that those people I mentioned make the road to hell so burdensome for themselves.

I: In what way?

HE: Why should they take on themselves the yoke of Christian love when it is not made either easy or meritorious for them by the dogmas?

I: Yes of course. This is a risk that we have to run. I only ask: Is it wise of certain other people, on account of this risk which these people run with their unchristian Christian love, to deny to them the name of Christians?

HE: *Cui non competit definitio, non competit definitum.* Have I invented that?

I: But suppose, nevertheless, we could interpret the definition a little more widely. We might follow the saying of a certain good man: "He who is not against us is for us." You know this good man?

HE: Very well. He is the same who in another place says: "He who is not with me is against me."

I: Yes indeed. Of course. That reduces me to silence. Oh, you alone are a true Christian. And as well read in the Scripture as the devil.

* * * * *

JEROME, *in Epist. ad Galatas, c. 6.*

Beatus Ioannes Evangelista, cum Ephesi moraretur usque ad ultimam senectutem, et vix inter discipulorum manus ad ecclesiam deferretur, nec posset in plura vocem verba contexere, nihil aliud per singulas solebat proferre collectas nisi hoc: Filioli diligite alterutrum. Tandem discipuli et fratres qui aderant, tædio affecti quod eadem semper audirent, dixerunt: Magister, quare semper hoc loqueris? Qui respondit dignam Ioanne sententiam: Quia præceptum Domini est, et si solum fiat sufficit.

III

NECESSARY ANSWER TO A VERY UNNECESSARY QUESTION OF HERR HAUPT-PASTOR GOEZE IN HAMBURG[1]

Wolfenbüttel, 1778

[Goeze objects to Lessing's assertion: "The Christian religion could exist even if the Bible were to become entirely lost, if it had long ago been entirely lost, if it had never existed." What, he asks, does Lessing mean when he speaks of "the Christian religion"? After an introduction, Lessing's reply proceeds as follows.]

1. The content of the Creed is called by the earliest Fathers *regula fidei*.

2. This *regula fidei* is not drawn from the writings of the New Testament.

3. This *regula fidei* existed before a single book of the New Testament existed.

4. This *regula fidei* is thus older than the Church. For the intention for which, the order under which, a community is gathered together, is certainly earlier than the community.

5. With this *regula fidei* not only were the first Christians, in the lifetime of the apostles, content; but also the succeeding Christians of the entire first four centuries considered it to be completely sufficient for Christianity.

6. This *regula fidei* is thus the rock on which the Church of Christ is built, and not the Scripture.

7. This *regula fidei* is the rock on which the Church of Christ is built and not Peter and his successors.

8. The writings of the New Testament, as contained in our present Canon, were not known to the first Christians, and the pieces which

[1] *Lessings Werke,* ed. Lachmann-Muncker, xiii, pp. 329–36.

62

they did happen to know were never held by them in the esteem which they have enjoyed among some of us since Luther's time.

9. The laity of the first Church were not allowed to read these pieces at all; at least, not without permission of the presbyter in whose charge they were.

10. It was even considered no small offence for the laity of the first Church to put more trust in the written words of an apostle than in the living word of their bishop.

11. In accordance with the *regula fidei* even the writings of the apostles were judged. The selection from their writings was made according to the degree of their agreement with the *regula fidei*, and writings were rejected according to the degree of their disagreement with it, even though their authors were, or were believed to be, apostles.

12. In the first four centuries the Christian religion was never proved out of the writings of the New Testament but was only explained and confirmed by the way, if at all.

13. The argument that the apostles and evangelists wrote their works with the intention that the Christian religion should be able to be completely concluded and proved from them, is not valid.

14. The argument that the Holy Ghost by his guidance, even without the intention of the writers, so ordered and arranged it, is still less valid.

15. The authenticity of the *regula fidei* can be proved far more easily and correctly than the authenticity of the New Testament writings.

16. By the undoubtedly proved authenticity of the *regula fidei* its divine nature can be proved with far greater certainty than the inspiration of the New Testament writings can be proved, as is now supposed, by their authenticity: This, in passing, is the daring step which makes the Librarian[1] so dissatisfied with all modern proofs of the truth of the Christian religion.

17. In the first centuries the writings of the apostles were not even regarded as an authentic commentary on the entire *regula fidei*.

18. And that was precisely the reason why the earliest Church would never allow the heretics to appeal to the Scripture. That was precisely the reason why they would never dispute with a heretic out of the Scripture.

[1] I.e. Lessing.

19. The entire true worth of the apostolic writings as regards the Creed is simply that they stand with the writings of the Christian teachers, and that, in so far as they agree with the *regula fidei*, they are the earliest examples of it, but not its sources.

20. The excess which they contain over and above the *regula fidei*, in the opinion of the first four centuries, is not necessary to salvation; it may be true or false; it may be interpreted one way or the other.

⋆   ⋆   ⋆   ⋆   ⋆

These propositions I have collected from my own careful and frequent, reading of the Church Fathers in the first four centuries, and I am in the position to enter into the most minute examination of the matter with the most learned patristic scholar. The best read student has in this question no more sources than I. The best read student can therefore know no more than I. And it is certainly not true that such deep and extended knowledge is required to reach the truth in all these matter as many perhaps imagine, and as many would have the world believe.

Perhaps I ought to add something further about the harmlessness of this my system, and at the same time show to advantage the particular use which the Christian religion can expect from it in facing its present enemies. But I shall have occasion for this in the further progression of the controversy; especially if Herr Haupt-pastor Goeze is willing to separate it from the rest of our little fight and to treat it without mixing it up with fresh slanders.

In order to make it easier for him, in this pamphlet I have carefully abstained from all parables, all illustrations, and all allusions.[1] And I am prepared to continue like this, if he is willing to use the same precision and simplicity in his Counter-propositions.[2]

[1] Goeze had complained that Lessing did not attack him in a straightforward manner, but bewildered his readers with metaphors, parables, and verbal ambiguities (cf. *Streitschriften*, ed. E. Schmidt, p. 5).

[2] Goeze's reply to this pamphlet reached Lessing from Elise Reimarus on 26 August 1778. He at once wrote a further reply as an appendix (*Der nöthige Antwort auf eine sehr unnöthige Frage*, Erste Folge, ed. Lachmann-Muncker, xiii, pp. 369–77). In this he argues (*a*) that the Roman Church refutes Goeze's assertion that all Christian teachers of all denominations hold the Bible to be the sole foundation of the Christian religion; and (*b*) that if it is made such there is no defence at all against the Socinians.

IV

NEW HYPOTHESIS CONCERNING THE EVANGELISTS REGARDED AS MERELY HUMAN HISTORIANS[1]

1778

1. CONTENTS

First the hypothesis will be set forth in plain, straightforward prose. Then the critical proof of it will be given, and all that follows on from it.

After this will be shown the advantage which this hypothesis could have in making intelligible various difficulties and in providing a more exact explanation of disputed passages, and the conclusion will subject it to a closer scrutiny.

2. PREFACE

This is the first draft of a work on which I have been working for many years. My intention was admittedly not to lay it before the world until it was quite complete. But circumstances have intervened which compel me to give a foretaste of it.

For I have been dragged into explaining certain matters which are very closely bound up with the present hypothesis. I may be astray here and there or in more than one place. Yet it will be found that where I have gone astray it is not because I have failed to use a map; I have always used the same map, which is denounced as more erroneous than careful measurement would bear out.

To hit on the right road is often pure luck. To be anxious to find the right road is alone praiseworthy.

Since, moreover, I have only spoken of a hypothesis, and I neither dispute nor deny the higher worth of the evangelists, this higher worth may very well stand secure even on my hypothesis. Thus I hope not to cause more shock or scandal than I intend to give. It goes without

[1] *Lessings Werke*, ed. Lachmann-Muncker, xvi, pp. 370-91.

saying that I acknowledge as my assessors and judges only those divines whose mind is as rich in cold critical learning as it is free from prejudices. I shall pay only little regard to the judgment of other members of this profession, however respectable they may seem to me on other grounds.

1. The first followers of Christ were pure Jews, and after Christ's example did not cease to live as Jews.* The other Jews gave them the name Nazarenes, for which I need merely refer to Acts xxiv. 5.

* For if there were also some Jewish proselytes among them, yet they were not merely proselytes of the Torah but proselytes of righteousness, who with circumcision had accepted the entire Mosaic law. Cf. Nicolas, Acts vi. 5.

2. Certainly the Jews may have given them this name out of scorn. But it was in profound accord with the mind of Christ's disciples that they did not reject a nickname which they had in common with their Master, but gladly accepted as an honourable title a name intended to discredit them.*

* Epiphanius says this expressly: οἱ τοῦ χριστοῦ μαθηταὶ . . . ἀκούοντες παρὰ ἄλλων Ναζωραῖοι, οὐκ ἠναίνοντο τὸν σκόπον θεωροῦντες τῶν τοῦτο αὐτοὺς καλούντων, ὅτι διὰ Χριστὸν αὐτοὺς ἐκαλοῦν. *Hæres*. xxix. 6, 7.

3. Therefore also there was nothing they could do to suppress this name again in a short time. Rather must we believe that even when the name "Christians" had been accepted in Antioch and for a long time been universal, the Palestinian Jewish Christians* would have preferred to keep their old name, Nazarenes, and would have been the more concerned to preserve it since it was convenient for distinguishing them from the uncircumcised Christians against whom they always had some slight hostility, many traces of which can be found in the New Testament.

* At least in part. For how else could it have happened that many centuries later in just the same region under just the same name a kind of Christians should have survived which confessed the same doctrines and lived in complete separation from the universal church which consisted chiefly of Gentiles?

4. Would it be safe to assume that those earliest Nazarenes, very early, very soon after the death of Christ, had a written collection of narratives concerning Christ's life and teaching, which arose out of orally transmitted stories of the apostles and all those people who had lived in association with Christ? Why not?*

* What here I merely postulate, will be shown in the sequel really to have

existed. One can have no conception of how curious the multitude is concerning every detail relating to a great man for whom they have once taken a fancy, if this postulate is to be disputed. And a multitude always swells to become a greater multitude: so it is natural that everything which can be learnt about the great man is passed from hand to hand; finally, when oral communication no longer suffices, it must be put into writing.

5. And how, speaking roughly, would this collection have appeared? Like a collection of narratives, the beginning of which is so small that the first originator can be forgotten without ingratitude; which by chance is enlarged by more than one and is copied by more than one with all the freedom that is usual with such works which are attributed to nobody—just as any other such collection, I say, would always appear. Basically it is always the same. But with each copy it is in some places enlarged, in some places abbreviated, in some places altered, according as the copyist or the possessor of the copy might believe that he had included more or better narratives from the mouths of credible people who had lived with Christ.*

* If we now, in modern times, have few or no examples of such historical narratives, like snowballs sometimes growing, sometimes melting away; the reason is that one or other of the first copies quickly receives its fixed form in writing by being printed. Anyone who has had frequent occasion to turn over the pages of ancient chronicles of great cities or distinguished families, will know to what extent every owner of a particular copy held himself to be permitted to exercise his right of possession, as often as he wished, even on the text, and would lengthen or abbreviate it.

6. And when at last the process of increasing or altering the collection had to stop, because at length the contemporaries whose authentic narratives anyone believed he could include inevitably died out; how would this collection then be entitled? Either, I imagine, after the first authorities for the narratives therein contained, or after those for whose use the collection would chiefly have been made; or after this or that man who first gave the collection an improved form or put it into a more intelligible language.

7. If it had been called after the first authorities, how would it have been entitled? The first authorities were all people who lived with Christ, and had known him to a greater or less degree. Among them were indeed a number of women, whose little anecdotes about Christ ought the less to be despised the greater the degree of their familiarity with him. But it was chiefly his apostles from whose mouth without

doubt the most numerous and reliable narratives originated. Thus it would have been entitled, this collection (the word Gospel taken in the sense of a historical narrative of Christ's life and teaching)—*The Gospel of the Apostles.*

8. And if they were named after those for whose use they were particularly made: how would they have been entitled then? How else than *The Gospel of the Nazarenes*? Or among those who did not wish to use the word Nazarenes *The Gospel of the Hebrews*. For this name quite properly belonged to the Nazarenes as Palestinian Jews.

9. Finally, if it had been named after this or that man who first gave it an improved form or translated it into a more intelligible language; how would it have been entitled then? How else than the Gospel of this man and that man, who had thus gained this credit?

10. Hitherto I shall seem to my readers to lose myself in pursuit of vain conjectures, whereas they expect something quite different from me. But only let them have patience. What seems to them so far to be vain conjectures is nothing else and nothing more than what I have abstracted from credible historical witnesses, which anyone else, who thought he could proceed less cautiously, might have used as an immediate proof of his assertion.

11. In fact we find that the Nazarenes of the fourth century not only desired to have, but actually had precisely such a collection of narratives concerning Christ and Christ's teaching. They had a Chaldaic-Syriac Gospel of their own which among the Church Fathers is mentioned sometimes under the name of the Gospel of the Apostles, sometimes the Gospel of the Hebrews, sometimes the Gospel of Matthew. The first title was given for the first reason explained in § 7; the second for the second reason in § 8; and the last *conjecturally* for the third reason of § 9.

12. I say conjecturally, and in my entire hypothesis this is the only conjecture that I allow myself and on which I build. It rests on so many grounds that no historical conjecture in the world could be found which more deserved to be accepted as historical truth.

13. And yet from this correspondence of the actual Gospel of the later Nazarenes of the fourth century with a merely hypothetical Gospel such as the very first Nazarenes must have had, if they had one at all, I do not at once draw the conclusion that the one must necessarily have been identical with the other. For it may be said that the later

Nazarenes were heretics and the very first Nazarenes were Jewish Christians of weak faith; thus the former could have put something together of which the latter knew nothing.

14. Let us therefore proceed as circumspectly as possible. Did any Church Father who mentioned the Gospel of the later Nazarenes ever express such a suspicion or even give any hint of it? Never. Not one.

15. Did not rather the most learned and acute Church Fathers always speak of it with a certain respect, not indeed as a Gospel inspired by the Holy Ghost but yet as an undoubtedly ancient work, written at or soon after the time of the apostles? Certainly.

16. Did not the same man, who was without doubt the only one of all the Church Fathers capable of using a Chaldaic-Syriac work, believe that on several occasions various passages from it could be used to explain the Greek text of the existing evangelists? Certainly. Jerome in fact.

17. Did not this same Jerome even translate it and think it worth translating into two different languages? He says so himself.

18. Why then is there reason to deny that the Gospel of the later Nazarenes was written by the first and most ancient Nazarenes? Is it not, rather, perfectly credible that the Syriac-Chaldaic Gospel, which in Jerome's age was in the hands of the Nazarenes or Ebionites of that time, may also have been in the hands of the Nazarenes at the time of the apostles, and that it may have been the written Gospel which the apostles themselves first used?

19. Admittedly the later Nazarenes were *called* heretics. But fundamentally they were no more heretics than the ancient Nazarenes to whom the name of heretics had not yet been given, as we may conclude from the silence of Irenæus. For both the one and the other believed that the Mosaic ceremonial law must be maintained together with Christianity.

20. That the later Nazarenes had no connection whatever with the earlier Nazarenes is a fancy notion of Mosheim in his youth when he audaciously attacked one Church Father in order to hit at the others as well. This the old and more cautious Mosheim himself denied.[1]

---

[1] J. L. Mosheim, *Vindiciæ antiquæ Christianorum disciplinæ contra Tolandi Nazarenum* (1719). See, for his later opinion, Mosheim's *Commentaries on the Affairs of the Christians before the Time of Constantine the Great* (tr. R. S. Vidal, London, 1813) ii, pp. 194 ff.

21. The minor disagreements, however, which even now can be observed in the extant fragments of the Nazarene Gospel, some of which are concerned with the same question, from which some might prefer to force the conclusion that the Ebionite and Nazarene Gospels were quite different, are rather to be explained from the manner of origin such as I have assumed to be probable in § 6. For since it could not occur to any ancient Nazarene to regard a work gradually compiled from various narratives as a divine book to which no subtraction or addition might be made, it was not surprising that the copies did not all agree.

22. If the Gospel of the Nazarenes was not an untimely birth substituted at a later date, it was even earlier than all our four gospels, the first of which was written at least thirty years after Christ's death.

23. Is it conceivable that in this thirty years there was no written record of Christ and his teaching? that the first person who decided to write one, after so long a time sat down to write it merely out of his or others' memories? that he had nothing before him by which he could justify himself in case he had to vindicate his statements in this or that detail? That is simply not credible even if he was inspired. For only he himself was aware of the inspiration, and probably even at that time people shrugged their shoulders over those who pretended to know historical facts by inspiration.

24. Thus there was a narrative of Christ written earlier than Matthew's. And during the thirty years it remained in that language in which alone its compilers could have written it. Or to put the matter less definitely and yet more accurately: it remained in the Hebrew language or in the Syriac-Chaldæan dialect of Hebrew as long as Christianity was for the most part still confined to Palestine and to the Jews in Palestine.

25. Only when Christianity was extended among the Gentiles, and so many who understood neither Hebrew nor a more modern dialect of it were curious to have better information about the person of Christ (which, however, may not have been during the first years of the Gentile mission, since all the first Gentile converts were content with the oral accounts which the apostles gave to each one), was it found necessary and useful to satisfy a pious curiosity by turning to that Nazarene source, and to make extracts or translations from it in a language which was the language of virtually the entire civilized world.

26. The first of these extracts, the first of these translations, was made, I think, by Matthew. And that, as I have said in § 12, is the conjecture which may boldly be included among the historical truths, if we have any of these things at all. For all that we know both of the person of Matthew and of his Gospel, or that we can reasonably assume, not only agrees completely with this conjecture; but also a great deal which is a recurrent problem that has been insoluble to many scholars can only be explained by this conjecture.

27. For in the first place Matthew is to be held without contradiction to be the first and earliest of our evangelists. But this, as already observed, cannot possibly mean that he was absolutely the first of all who put anything into writing about Christ which was in the hands of the new converts. It can only mean that he was the first who wrote in Greek.

28. Secondly, it is very probable that Matthew was the only apostle who understood Greek, without needing to receive knowledge of this language directly through the Holy Ghost.

29. Thirdly, in favour of this view is the occasion on which Matthew must have composed his Gospel. For Eusebius writes (*H. E.* iii. 24. 5): "Matthew for some years preached the Gospel to the Hebrews in Palestine; when he finally decided to go to others for this purpose, he left his Gospel in writing in his mother tongue, so that even in his absence he might remain their teacher."* Of this strictly speaking only half can be true. Only the occasion on which Matthew wrote his Gospel can be right. But this occasion was not that he had to write a *Hebrew* Gospel, but rather that he thought a Greek compilation to be required. That is: when he had preached for long enough to the Hebrews, he did not leave behind for the Hebrews his Gospel in Hebrew (among the Hebrews in Palestine there still remained many apostles whose oral instruction they could have at any moment), but for his future use, since he now intended to preach the Gospel to others who did not understand Hebrew, he made from the Hebrew *Gospel of the Apostles* a selection in the language understood by the majority.

* This may be the place to emend a passage of Jerome. In the introduction to his Commentary on Matthew Jerome says: "Primus omnium (*sc.* Evangelistarum) Matthæus est, qui Evangelium in Judæa hebræo sermone edidit, ob eorum vel maxime causam, qui in Jesum crediderunt ex Judæis et *nequaquam*

legis umbram, succedente Evangelii veritate, servabant." They observed the shadow of the law *in no way whatever (nequaquam)*? But the first Jews in Judæa to become Christians certainly remained in obstinate adherence to the law. I think therefore that here, for *nequaquam* we should read *nequicquam, incassum,* "in vain," "to no purpose."

And that Matthew really wrote for the Nazarenes, that is for Jewish Christians who wanted to associate Moses and Christ, is to be seen from chapter v. 17–20, where he attributes words to Jesus found in no other evangelist, and which no doubt must have made the Nazarenes obstinate. Especially verse 17, where it is ridiculous, instead of the Mosaic law in general, to understand the moral law alone. The exposition of the Babylonian Talmud is indisputably right. See the English Bible.[1] We have now of course reason, indeed we can claim the right, to expound this passage differently. But should fault be found with the first Jewish Christians if they understood it in this way?

Similarly Mark and Luke have left out the command which according to Matthew x. 5–6, the Saviour gave his disciples whom he sent out to heal and to do miracles.

30. Fourthly, the entire controversy concerning the original language of Matthew is settled in a way which can satisfy both parties: both those who, following the unanimous testimony of the Church Fathers, assert that the original language of Matthew's Gospel was Hebrew; and also the modern Protestant dogmatic theologians who have and must needs have their objections to this view.

31. Indeed, the original of Matthew was certainly Hebrew, but Matthew himself was not the actual author of this original. From him, as an apostle, many narratives in the Hebrew original may well derive. But he himself did not commit these narratives to writing. At his dictation others wrote them down in Hebrew and combined them with stories from the other apostles; and from this human collection he in his time made merely a connected selection in Greek. But because his selection, his translation, followed quickly on the original, because he himself could equally well have written in Hebrew, because in view of his personal circumstances it was more probable that he in fact wrote in Hebrew, it is not surprising that to some extent the original was confused with the translation.

32. And everyone will recognize how much may be gained from accepting this view by the modern divines who from the internal

[1] *Die heilige Schrift . . . nebst einer vollständigen Erklärung derselben, welche aus den auserlesensten Anmerkungen verschiedener Engländischen Schriftsteller zusammengetragen, übersetzt von J. D. Heyde, herausgegeben von Romanus Teller, J. A. Dietelmair und Jakob Brucker* (Leipzig, 1749–70, 19 vols.).

evidence of Matthew and for not inconsiderable dogmatic reasons think we must conclude that Matthew could not have written in any language other than that in which we now have him. Matthew wrote what he wrote in Greek; but he drew it from a Hebrew source.

33. If he made this selection in a better known language with all the diligence, with all the caution, of which such an enterprise is worthy, then indeed, to speak only humanly, a good spirit assisted him. And no one can object if one calls this good spirit the Holy Spirit. And in this way must Matthew have gone to work; such a good spirit must have guided and supported him. For his selection or his translation not only attained rapidly to canonical rank among the Christians generally, but even among the Nazarenes themselves the name of the Greek translator henceforth became attached to the Hebrew original, and this itself was given out to be a work of Matthew. The Gospel *secundum Apostolos* came in time to be called by most people the Gospel *juxta Matthæum*, as Jerome expressly says.

34. That I have not drawn a false conclusion here is shown by the long threads that do not snap, which I am in a position to unwind from a very tangled ball. That is: from this suggestion of mine I can explain twenty things which remain insoluble problems if one or other of the usual assertions about the original language of Matthew is maintained. I mention the most important, because in critical matters, as is well known, the new solutions which a fresh hypothesis provides, are equal to proofs of its truth.

35. When Epiphanius for example says that the Nazarenes possessed the Gospel of Matthew τὸ πληρέστατον Ἑβραϊστί "quite complete in Hebrew" [*Panar.* xxix. 9. 4]: what can be said about this which avoids all objections? Was it Matthew himself who wrote this complete Hebrew text? Then our Greek Matthew is not complete. If Matthew originally wrote in Greek, then in their version the Nazarenes added human additions to it, which they would not have done if it had stood in the canonical honour which it now possesses. And how could Origen and Jerome treat these additions so indulgently? Only after my interpretation of this matter have Epiphanius' words their proper force. The Hebrew original of Matthew contained more than Matthew thought good to extract for his Greek selection. The overplus which was in the Hebrew Matthew was not interpolated by the later Nazarenes, but was omitted by Matthew.

36. Likewise, who can answer the following? If Matthew wrote originally in Greek, how does it come about that the Church Fathers unanimously assert that his Gospel was composed in Hebrew? And if he wrote his Gospel originally in Hebrew, how could his original Hebrew text be allowed to become lost? Who, I ask, can give so satisfactory an answer to this as I? The Church Fathers found a Hebrew Gospel which contained everything in Matthew and more. They thus believed it to be Matthew's own work. But this Hebrew text, supposed to be Matthew's, was in fact as regards its historical content the source of Matthew. But only the Greek selection was the actual work of the apostle, who wrote under higher oversight. Why then did it happen that the material he used was lost, after it had been used in the most authoritative way?

37. Nothing, however, more confirms my opinion that Matthew did not write in Hebrew but only translated and used a Hebrew original so faithfully and carefully that the original itself was given his name—nothing, I say, more confirms this opinion than the fact that it makes intelligible a sentence of Papias which has caused innumerable commentators so much ungrateful trouble. Papias says, according to Eusebius: Ματθαῖος μὲν οὖν Ἑβραΐδι διαλέκτῳ τὰ λόγια ουνεγράψατο, ἡρμήνευσε δ' αὐτὰ ὡς ἦν δυνατὸς ἕκαστος "Matthew wrote his Gospel in Hebrew; but each man translated it as well as he could".

38. The last words of this passage are admittedly so difficult that people have thought they must deny to the good Papias all credit in respect of the first. They have not been able to imagine that in these words Papias really intended to say what they so obviously do say. In particular it is very amusing to see what trimming Clericus[1] gives him here, and how like a schoolmaster he corrected the Greek words for the Greek, without considering that he is schoolmastering not so much Papias as Eusebius, or at least Eusebius just as much as Papias (for every writer must also be responsible for the words he quotes from someone else, in so far as they appear to contain nonsense, if he passes them without a syllable of censure).

[1] J. Le Clerc of Amsterdam (1657–1736) was an acute Protestant scholar. In his *Harmony of the Evangelists* (E. T., 1701, pp. 603 ff.) he attacks Papias' credit, especially criticizing his famous sentence about Matthew, in an argument against Richard Simon's view that the Gospel of the Nazarenes was the original of Matthew.

39. As I have said, of course one has reason to attack Papias and to ask him whether he knew what he was saying by ὡς ἠδύνατο ἕκαστος. Did he mean that our Greek Matthew was not such a good translation as any version could be? Or that in reality there existed several Greek translations of his Hebrew Matthew? If so, how does it come about that of these several translations there is nowhere the smallest trace? We cannot tell what Papias might answer to these questions.

40. But now assume with me that Papias had in mind not an original Hebrew Matthew, but the Hebrew original of Matthew, which, because Matthew had been the first to make it generally known and usable, thenceforward circulated under his name. What absurdity is there then when Papias says that nevertheless many still turned to the Hebrew original and produced new versions of it in Greek?

41. Have we not already seen that Matthew was not a mere translator of anything and everything which he found in the Gospel of the Nazarenes? He left much which was not familiar to him, though it had good authority. There were stories which originated from all eleven apostles; many of them were quite true but were not sufficiently useful for the later Christian world. There were stories which originated only from Christ's women associates, of which it was in part doubtful whether they had always understood correctly the wonder-man whom they so loved. There were stories which could only have come from his mother, from people who had known him in his childhood at the house of his parents; and however reliable they were, what help could they be to the world, which had enough to learn of what he did and said after entering upon his teaching office?

42. What was thus more natural? Since Matthew's translation could not be stamped with any unmistakable sign of divinity, and since it only attained canonical status through examination and comparison, and so was confirmed by the Church and preserved—what was more natural than that several others who either did not know or did not entirely approve of Matthew's work, because they wished it contained this or that story, or because they would have preferred this or that story to be told differently, should undertake the same work, and should carry it out as each individual's powers enabled him? ὡς ἠδύνατο ἕκαστος.

43. And thus we stand here at the source from which flowed forth both the better Gospels that are still extant and the less good ones which on that account fell out of use and so were finally lost.*

* It is a completely mistaken notion to suppose that the heretics forged false Gospels. On the contrary, because there were so many Gospels which all originated from the one Nazarene source, there were so many heretics, each one of whom has as much in his favour as any other.

It is, for example, not less than credible that Cerinthus made his own Gospel. He had nothing more than his own translation of the Hebrew original of Matthew.

Jerome says this expressly (*Prooem. in Comment. super Matth.*): "Plures fuisse qui Evangelia scripserunt, et Lucas Evangelista testatur dicens: quandoquidem— et perseverantia usque in præsens tempus monimenta declarant, quæ a diversis autoribus edita, diversarum hæreseon fuere principia." Thus the different Gospels were not the work of heretics, but the fact that there were so many Gospels caused so many heresies to come into existence.

So also says Epiphanius (*Hæres.* lxii) of the Sabellians, that they constructed their entire error out of the false Gospels: τὴν δὲ πᾶσαν αὐτῶν πλάνην ἔχουσιν ἐξ ἀποκρύφων τινῶν, μάλιστα ἀπὸ τοῦ καλουμένου Αἰγυπτίου εὐαγγελίου.

44. That there were many Gospels of this second kind, even if we did not know it from Church history, we should have to believe entirely on the evidence of Luke alone, who indeed could not have had in mind the entirely fictitious invented Gospels and apostolic writings of the heretics,* but must necessarily have had in mind Gospels whose original matter was unexceptionable, but whose order, arrangement, and purpose was not entirely straightforward and clear, when he says that through them he was encouraged and felt entitled also to write a history of the Lord.

* "Epiphanius and Ambrose think Luke may here refer to the Gospels of the heretics Basilides, Cerinthus, and others, as has already been noted by Daniel Heinsius (*Exercit. sacr.*, lib. 3, ch. 1)."—Masch, § 30.[1]

"Ausus fuit et Basilides scribere evangelium et suo illud nomine titulare," writes Origen (*Homilia I in Lucam*). Ambrose also says the same (*Comment. in S. Lucam*). And Jerome, in the Preface to his *Commentary on St. Matthew*. But Basilides lived in the second century: how could Luke have had his Gospel in mind? If indeed Basilides actually wrote one, and Ambrose and Jerome are not merely copying Origen who probably made the assertion without foundation! (See Mosheim, *Comment. de Rebus Christianorum ante Constant. Magnum*, p. 357.) But not one of all these says that Luke was referring to it; they only mention this Gospel in commenting on Luke's text; and that is a nasty tumble for Herr Masch.

In the case of Cerinthus it is more possible that Luke was referring to it. And Epiphanius (*Adversus Hæres.* li. 428) seems to make it certain. But as

[1] Daniel Heinsius (1580–1655), *Exercitationes sacræ ad Novum Testamentum* (Leiden, 1639); Andreas Gottlieb Masch (1724–1807), *Abhandlung von der Grundsprache des Evangelii Matthäi* (Halle, 1755).

Epiphanius in another place says that he only accepted Matthew's Gospel, the Gospel of Cerinthus was thus nothing but his own translation of the Hebrew original.

In general I certainly find evidence that the heretics were accused of falsifying the Gospel history; though not so often as people imagine, for Origen says (*Contra Celsum*, ii. 5. 27) that this had only been done by the pupils of Marcion, of Valentinus, and if I do not err, he adds, of Lucan. But that the heretics forged entire Gospels out of their own heads I can find no evidence. Their Gospels were also ancient narratives circulating under the names of the apostles or apostolic men. Only they were not those which were generally accepted in the Church. They had indeed the source in common with these; but the man who drew on this source was less reliable.

45. I might even be inclined to believe that in the passage of Luke now in question the Hebrew source is expressly mentioned, and by its title which may well have been (in Hebrew, of course) διήγησις περὶ τῶν πεπληροφορημένων ἐν ἡμῖν πραγμάτων.* It may be that the following words, καθὼς παρέδοσαν ἡμῖν οἱ ἀπ'ἀρχῆς αὐτόπται καὶ ὑπηρέται τοῦ λόγου, were included in the title or were only added by Luke to give a much clearer designation of the authentic collection.**

* That is: "Narrative of the things which have been fulfilled among us." A title which I think has a quite Hebraic ring, although I cannot myself or with the help of others declare how it could have been expressed in Syriac or Chaldæan. Probably this would be a reference to the numerous prophecies fulfilled by the events of the teaching and acts of Christ. Cf. the frequently recurring τοῦτο δὲ γέγονεν ἵνα πληρωθῇ τὸ ῥηθὲν ὑπὸ τοῦ κυρίου διὰ τοῦ προφήτου (Matt. i. 22; ii. 17; iv. 14; viii. 17; xii. 17; xiii. 14).

** In both cases this confirms what I have said in general in §§ 2–4 of the people who so to speak contributed to the writing of the Gospel of the Nazarenes. ὑπηρέται τοῦ λόγου are the apostles, as the most eminent after whom the whole collection was named; and αὐτόπται are all those men and women who knew Christ personally.

46. And if accordingly I translate the entire first clause of Luke ἐπειδήπερ πολλοὶ ἐπεχείρησαν ἀνατάξασθαι διήγησιν περὶ τῶν πεπληροφορημένων ἐν ἡμῖν πραγμάτων "Quoniam quidem multi conati sunt, *iterum iterumque* in ordinem redigere narrationem *illam* de rebus quæ in nobis completæ sunt": what objections could be urged against it?*

* At any rate to translate ἀνατάξασθαι διήγησιν merely by *litteris mandare*, merely by "write," "compose," seems to me not fully to represent the meaning of the words. For ἀνα seems here also to signify a frequent repetition, which

fits in especially with ἐπεχείρησαν, "they have taken in hand." Consequently I
would prefer to render it: "Because many have repeatedly attempted to arrange
in order that narrative concerning the things fulfilled among us, so . . ." etc.
The task of arranging in order the ancient collection which had arisen so
casually out of such various narratives was without doubt the more difficult.
The translating of it, once agreement had been reached about the order, was
indisputably the easier task. Thus we need not be surprised that Luke speaks
only of the more difficult part in referring to the entire work.

Admittedly all this would be even more probable if τὴν stood before
διήγησιν.

47. Indeed, although I only put forward this translation and explanation as a critical conjecture, which is far less bold and adventurous than
critical conjectures usually are in these days, yet it seems to me that
only this view can deal with all the difficulties which can be raised
against Luke's words.*

* For if according to the usual translation he says: "Since many have ventured
to draw up an account of the events which have happened among us, as it has
been passed on to us by those who from the beginning have been eyewitnesses
and ministers of the Word"; have we not the right to interrupt Luke at once
saying: "Have those many written nothing except in accord with the information of the eyewitnesses and first ministers of the Word? And if so, beloved
Luke, what need is there of your work which all the labour you have bestowed
upon it cannot make an improvement? Have you ascertained everything yourself from the beginning? Are you able to give a better testimony than the story
'as it has been passed on to us by those who from the beginning have been
eyewitnesses and ministers of the Word'?" Only if these last words were
either part of the title of the first Hebrew document or were added by Luke to
designate it more closely and accurately, so that they refer to the Hebrew
document itself and not to the ordering and translating undertaken by many,
had Luke the right to undertake a similar work after he had ascertained
everything from the beginning, i.e. after he had examined and confirmed
everything which stood in the Hebrew document by comparison with the
oral declarations of the apostles with whom he had had opportunity for
conversation.

48. Yet be that as it may. It is enough that so much is certain, that
Luke himself had before him the Hebrew document, the Gospel of the
Nazarenes, and transferred, if not everything, at least most of the con-
tents to his Gospel, only in a rather different order and in rather better
language.

49. It is still more obvious that Mark, who is commonly held to be
only an abbreviator of Matthew, appears to be so only because he

drew upon the same Hebrew document, but probably had before him a less complete copy.*

* That he in fact drew immediately upon the Hebrew document is shown by chapter v. 41, where he includes the actual Chaldæan words which Christ used when raising Jairus' daughter, which neither Matthew nor Luke have. Also vii. 1, Corban.
Mark must have been the interpreter and trusted disciple of Peter. This without doubt explains the fact that he omits what Matthew relates of Peter in xiv. 28–31. On the other hand, it is much more difficult to conceive why he also omitted what Matthew relates of Peter in xvi. 17, although he (Mark) preserves viii. 33.

50. In short, Matthew, Mark, and Luke are simply different and not different translations of the so-called Hebrew document of Matthew which everyone interpreted as well as he could: ὡς ἠδύνατο ἕκαστος.

51. And John? It is quite certain that John knew and read that Hebrew document, and used it in his Gospel. Nevertheless his Gospel is not to be reckoned with the others, it does not belong to the Nazarene class. It belongs to a class all of its own.

52. The opinion that John intended to write a mere supplement to the other three Gospels is certainly unfounded. One need only read him to receive quite another impression.[1]

53. That John did not know the other three Gospels at all is both unprovable and incredible.

54. Rather, just because he had read the other three and several other Gospels originating from the Nazarene document, and because he saw the effect of these Gospels, he found himself impelled to write his Gospel.

55. For we need only remind ourselves of the actual origins of the Gospel of the Nazarenes—from honest people who had had personal converse with Christ, and who thus must have been completely convinced of Christ as man, and apart from Christ's own words, which they had more faithfully impressed upon their memory than clearly grasped in their understanding, could not relate anything about him which could not have been true of a mere man, though doing miracles by an endowment of power from on high.

56. Is it therefore surprising that not only the Palestinian Jewish Christians to whom the name Nazarenes particularly applied, but all

[1] Lessing intended to add footnotes to this proposition, but they are lost.

the Jews and Gentiles who had drawn their knowledge of Christ directly or indirectly from the Nazarene document, did not pay sufficient reverence to Christ in respect of his Godhead?

57. The former, even if our consideration goes back to their origins, could not possibly have intended to keep also the Mosaic law if they had regarded Christ as more than an extraordinary prophet. Indeed, even though they held him to be the true, promised Messiah, and as Messiah called him Son of God; yet it is beyond dispute that they did not mean by this title a Son of God who is of the same essence as God.

58. If anyone has doubts whether to concede this of the first Jewish Christians, he must at least grant that the Ebionites, that is, those Jewish Christians who before the destruction of Jerusalem escaped to Pella on the other side of Jordan, and even in the fourth century acknowledged no other Gospel than the Hebrew original of Matthew —that the Ebionites, I say, according to Origen's testimony, held a very poor opinion of Christ, even if it is not true that they received their name from the poverty of their way of thinking.

59. So also Cerinthus, who was certainly a Jew but hardly a Palestinian Jew because he was reckoned among the Gnostics, believed Christ to be simply the natural Son of Joseph and Mary born in the normal course of nature, because he accepted either the Hebrew original of Matthew or the Greek Matthew for the only Gospel (though he may have accepted it as such because he held this view).*

* In view of what I have said in the note to § 44, it seems to me quite credible that he made his own version of the Hebrew original, and so belonged himself to those in Papias who translated Matthew as well as they could.

60. The same is true of Carpocrates who similarly either could not hold any higher idea of Christ because he only accepted Matthew, or could only accept Matthew because he believed he should hold no higher idea of Christ.

61. In a word: Orthodox and Sectaries all had of the divine person of Christ either no idea at all or a quite wrong idea, as long as there existed no other Gospel but the Hebrew document of Matthew or the Greek Gospels which flowed from it.

62. If therefore Christianity was not to die down again and to disappear among the Jews as a mere Jewish sect, and if it was to endure

among the Gentiles as a separate, independent religion, John must come forward and write his Gospel.

63. It was only his Gospel which gave the Christian religion its true consistency. We have only his Gospel to thank if the Christian religion, despite all attacks, continued in this consistency and will probably survive as long as there are men who think they need a mediator between themselves and the Deity; that is, for ever.

64. That we accordingly have only two Gospels, Matthew and John, the Gospel of the flesh and the Gospel of the spirit, was long ago recognized by the early Church Fathers, and is actually denied by no modern orthodox theologian.

65. And now I would only have to explain how it came about that the Gospel of the flesh was proclaimed by three evangelists if I had not already explained it. For to speak more precisely, I would only have to explain why among many other Greek Gospels which originated from the Nazarene document, the Church only preserved Mark and Luke in addition to Matthew; for the reason given by Augustine for this is scarcely satisfactory.

66. I will give my opinion briefly. Mark and Luke were preserved by the Church in addition to Matthew because in many respects they filled so to speak the gap between Matthew and John; and the one was a pupil of Peter and the other a pupil of Paul.

67. That, I say, is my opinion which provides an adequate reason why the four evangelists were put together in almost all ancient copies without variation. For it has not been shown that they must have been written in precise chronological order one after another.

68. But here I cannot produce the argument supporting this opinion because I must proceed by induction, and I have been unable to put enough examples together to give this induction the probability of demonstration.

V

THE EDUCATION OF THE HUMAN RACE

"Hæc omnia inde esse in quibusdam vera, unde in quibusdam
falsa sunt."

AUGUSTINE

EDITED BY GOTTHOLD EPHRAIM LESSING

EDITOR'S PREFACE

I have published the first half of this essay in my *Contributions*. Now
I am in a position to give the remainder.

The author has set himself upon a high eminence from which he
believes it possible to see beyond the limits of the allotted path of his
present day's journey.

But he does not call away from his road any wanderer hastening
home whose one desire is to reach his night's logding. He does not ask
that the view which enchants him should also enchant every other eye.

And so, I would suppose, he may be allowed to stand and wonder
where he stands and wonders.

Would that from the immeasurable distance which a soft evening
glow neither entirely conceals nor wholly reveals to his gaze, he could
bring some guiding hint, for which I have often felt myself at a loss!

This is what is in my mind. Why are we not more willing to see in
all positive religions simply the process by which alone human understanding in every place can develop and must still further develop,
instead of either ridiculing or becoming angry with them? In the best
world there is nothing that deserves this scorn, this indignation we
show. Are the religions alone to deserve it? Is God to have part in
everything except our mistakes?

THE EDUCATION OF THE HUMAN RACE[1]

1. What education is to the individual man, revelation is to the whole
human race.

[1] F. W. Robertson's translation (1858) has been used as the basis of the present
version, but has been drastically revised.

2. Education is revelation coming to the individual man; and revelation is education which has come, and is still coming, to the human race.

3. Whether it can be of any advantage to the science of instruction to consider education from this point of view I will not here inquire; but in theology it may unquestionably be of great advantage, and may remove many difficulties, if revelation be conceived of as an education of the human race.

4. Education gives man nothing which he could not also get from within himself; it gives him that which he could get from within himself, only quicker and more easily. In the same way too, revelation gives nothing to the human race which human reason could not arrive at on its own; only it has given, and still gives to it, the most important of these things sooner.

5. And just as in education, it is not a matter of indifference in what order the powers of a man are developed, as it cannot impart to a man everything at once; so also God had to maintain a certain order and a certain measure in his revelation.

6. Even though the first man was furnished at once with a conception of the One God; yet it was not possible that this conception, freely imparted and not won by experience, should subsist long in its clearness. As soon as human reason, left to itself, began to elaborate it, it broke up the one immeasurable into many measurables, and gave a distinguishing mark to every one of these parts.

7. Hence naturally arose polytheism and idolatry. And who can say for how many millions of years human reason would have been lost in these errors, even though at all places and times there were individual men who recognized them *as* errors, had it not pleased God to afford it a better direction by means of a new impulse?

8. But when he neither could, nor would, reveal himself any more to *each* individual man, he selected an individual people for his special education; and that the most rude and the most ferocious, in order to begin with it from the very beginning.

9. This was the Hebrew people, about whom we do not even know what kind of divine worship they had in Egypt. For so despised a race of slaves could not have been permitted to take part in the worship of the Egyptians; and the God of their fathers had become entirely unknown to them.

10. It is possible that the Egyptians had expressly prohibited the Hebrews from having a god or gods, and having destroyed their faith, had brought them to the belief that they had no god or gods whatsoever; that to have a god or gods was the prerogative only of the superior Egyptians; this perhaps in order to be able to tyrannize over them with a greater show of fairness. Do Christians treat their slaves much differently even now?

11. To this rude people God caused himself to be announced at first simply as "the God of their fathers," in order to make them familiar and at home with the idea of a God belonging to them too.

12. Following this, through the miracles with which he led them out of Egypt and planted them in Canaan, he testified of himself to them as a God mightier than any other god.

13. And as he continued demonstrating himself to be the mightiest of all, which only one can be, he gradually accustomed them to the idea of the One.

14. But how far was this conception of the One below the true transcendental conception of the One, which reason, so late, teaches us only to conclude with certainty out of the conception of the infinite!

15. Although the best of the people were already more or less approaching the true conception of the One, the people as a whole could not for a long time elevate themselves to it. And this was the sole reason why they so often abandoned their one God, and expected to find the One, i.e. the mightiest, in some other god belonging to another people.

16. But of what kind of moral education was a people so raw, so incapable of abstract thoughts, and so entirely in their childhood, capable? Of none other but such as is adapted to the age of children, an education by rewards and punishments addressed to the senses.

17. Here too, then, education and revelation come together. As yet God could give to his people no other religion, no other law than one through obedience to which they might hope to be happy, or through disobedience to which they must fear to be unhappy. For as yet they envisaged nothing beyond this life. They knew of no immortality of the soul; they yearned after no life to come. But now to reveal these things, when their reason was so little prepared for them, what would it have been but the same fault in the divine rule as is committed by

the vain schoolmaster who chooses to hurry his pupil too rapidly and boast of his progress, rather than thoroughly to ground him?

18. "But," it will be asked, "to what purpose was this education of so rude a people, a people with whom God had to begin so entirely from the beginning?" I reply: "In order that in the process of time he might all the better employ particular members of this nation as the teachers of all other peoples. He was bringing up in them the future teachers of the human race. These were Jews, these could only be Jews, only men from a people which had been educated in this way."

19. Then further. When the child by dint of blows and caresses had grown and was now come to years of understanding, the Father sent it of a sudden into foreign lands: and here it recognized at once the good which in its Father's house it had possessed, and had not been conscious of.

20. While God guided his chosen people through all the degrees of a child's education, the other nations of the earth had gone on by the light of reason. The most part had remained far behind the chosen people. Only a few had got in front of them. And this, too, takes place with children, who are allowed to grow up on their own; many remain quite raw; some educate themselves to an astonishing degree.

21. But as these more fortunate few prove nothing against the use and necessity of education, so the few heathen nations, who hitherto seemed to be ahead of the chosen people even in the knowledge of God, prove nothing against a revelation. The child of education begins with slow but sure footsteps; it is late in overtaking many a more happily placed child of nature; but it *does* overtake it; and thenceforth can never be overtaken by it again.

22. Similarly—putting aside the doctrine of the unity of God, which in a way is found, and in a way is not found, in the books of the Old Testament—the fact that the doctrine of immortality at least is not to be found in it, but is wholly foreign to it, and all the related doctrine of reward and punishment in a future life, proves just as little against the divine origin of these books. For let us suppose that these doctrines were not only wanting there, but even that they were not even true; let us suppose that for mankind all was over in this life; would the being of God be for this reason less demonstrated? Would God on this account be less at liberty, would it less become him, to take immediate charge of the temporal fortunes of any people out of this perishable

race? The miracles which he performed for the Jews, the prophecies which he caused to be recorded through them, were surely not for the few mortal Jews, in whose time they happened and were recorded: his intentions there concerned the whole Jewish people, the entire human race, who, perhaps, are destined to remain for ever here on earth, even though every individual Jew and every individual man dies and is gone for ever.

23. Once more, the absence of those doctrines in the writings of the Old Testament proves nothing against their divinity. Moses was sent from God even though the sanction of his law extended only to this life. For why should it extend further? He was surely sent only to the Israelitish people, to the Israelitish people *of that time*, and his commission was perfectly adapted to the knowledge, capacities, inclinations of the *then existing* Israelitish people, as well as to the destiny of the people that was to come. And this is sufficient.

24. So far ought Warburton to have gone, and no further. But that learned man overdrew his bow. Not content that the absence of these doctrines did not *discredit* the divine mission of Moses, it must even be a *proof* to him of the divinity of the mission. If he had only sought this proof in the suitability of such a law for such a people!

But he took refuge in the hypothesis of a miraculous system continued in an unbroken line from Moses to Christ, according to which God had made every individual Jew just as happy or unhappy as his obedience or disobedience to the law deserved. This miraculous system, he said, had compensated for the lack of those doctrines [of eternal rewards and punishments] without which no state can subsist; and precisely this compensation proved what that lack at first sight appeared to deny.

25. How well it was that Warburton could by no argument prove or even make likely this continuous miracle, in which he placed the essence of the Israelitish theocracy! For could he have done so, then indeed, but not until then, he would have made the difficulty really insuperable, for me at least. For the truth which the divinity of Moses' mission was to restore, would, in fact, have been actually made doubtful by it: a truth which God, it is true, did not at that time want to reveal; but which, on the other hand, he certainly did not wish to make harder of attainment.

26. I will illustrate by something that is a counterpart to the process of revelation. A primer for children may fairly pass over in silence this or that important piece of the science or art which it expounds, when the teacher considers that it is not yet suitable for the capabilities of the children for whom he was writing. But it must contain absolutely nothing which bars the way to the knowledge which is held back, or which misleads the children away from it. Rather, all the approaches towards it must be carefully left open; and to lead them away from even one of these approaches, or to cause them to enter it later than they need, would alone be enough to change the mere imperfection of the primer into an actual fault.

27. In the same way, in the writings of the Old Testament, those primers for the Israelitish people, rough, unpractised in thought as they are, the doctrines of the immortality of the soul, and future recompense, might be fairly left out: but they were bound to contain nothing which could even have delayed the progress of the people for whom they were written, in their way to this great truth. And what, to say the least, could have delayed them more than the promise of such a miraculous recompense in this life—promised by him who makes no promise that he does not keep?

28. For even if the strongest proof of the immortality of the soul and of a life to come were not to be alleged from the inequality of the distribution of the material rewards in this life, in which so little account appears to be taken of virtue and vice; yet it is at least certain that without this difficulty—to be resolved in the life to come— human reason would still be far from any better and firmer proofs, and perhaps even would never have reached them. For what was to impel it to seek for these better proofs? Mere curiosity?

29. An Israelite here and there, no doubt, might have extended to every individual member of the entire state those promises and threatenings which applied to it as a whole, and been firmly persuaded that whosoever is pious must also be happy, and that whoever was unhappy must be bearing the penalty of his wrong-doing, which penalty would at once change itself into blessing, as soon as he aban- doned his sin. One like this appears to have written Job, for the plan of it is entirely in this spirit.

30. But it was impossible that daily experience should confirm this conviction, or else it would have been all over, for ever, with the

people who had this experience, so far as all recognition and reception were concerned of the truth as yet unfamiliar to them. For if the pious man were absolutely happy, and it was also a necessary part of his happiness that his satisfaction should be broken by no uneasy thoughts of death, and that he should die old and "full of days"[1]: how could he yearn for another life? and how could he reflect upon a thing for which he did not yearn? But if the pious did not reflect on it, who then should reflect? The transgressor? he who felt the punishment of his misdeeds, and if he cursed this life must have so gladly renounced that other existence?

31. It was of much less consequence that an Israelite here and there should directly and expressly have denied the immortality of the soul and future recompense, on the grounds that the law had no reference to it. The denial of an individual, had it even been a Solomon,[2] did not arrest the progress of the common reason, and was in itself, even, a proof that the nation had now taken a great step nearer to the truth. For individuals only deny what the many are thinking over; and to think over an idea about which before no one troubled himself in the least, is half-way to knowledge.

32. Let us also acknowledge that it is a heroic obedience to obey the laws of God simply because they are God's laws, and not because he has promised to reward those who obey them now and hereafter; to obey them even though there be an entire despair of future recompense, and uncertainty respecting a temporal one.

33. Must not a people educated in this heroic obedience towards God be destined, must they not be capable beyond all others of executing divine purposes of quite a special character? Let the soldier, who pays blind obedience to his leader, also become convinced of his leader's wisdom, and then say what that leader may not venture to do with his aid.

34. As yet the Jewish people had worshipped in their Jehovah rather the mightiest than the wisest of all gods; as yet they had rather feared him as a jealous God than loved him: this, too, is a proof that the conceptions which they had of their eternal One God were not exactly the right conceptions which we should have of God. However, now the time was come for these conceptions of theirs to be expanded,

[1] Cf. Genesis xxv. 8; xxxv. 29.
[2] Ecclesiastes iii. 19–21.

ennobled, rectified, to accomplish which God availed himself of a perfectly natural means, a better and more correct measure, by which they got the opportunity of appreciating him.

35. Instead of, as hitherto, appreciating him in contrast with the miserable idols of the small neighbouring peoples, with whom they lived in constant rivalry, they began, in captivity under the wise Persians, to measure him against the "Being of all Beings" such as a more disciplined reason recognized and worshipped.

36. Revelation had guided their reason, and now, all at once, reason gave clearness to their revelation.

37. This was the first reciprocal influence which these two (reason and revelation) exercised on one another; and so far is such a mutual influence from being unbecoming to the author of them both, that without it either of them would have been useless.

38. The child, sent into foreign lands, saw other children who knew more, who lived more becomingly, and asked itself, in confusion, "Why do I not know that too? Why do I not live so too? Ought I not to have learnt and acquired all this in my Father's house?" Thereupon it again sought out its primer, which had long been thrown into a corner, in order to push the blame on to the primer. But behold, it discovers that the blame does not rest upon books, but the blame is solely its own, for not having long ago known this very thing, and lived in this very way.

39. Since the Jews, by this time, through the medium of the pure Persian doctrine, recognized in their Jehovah not simply the greatest of all national deities, but God; and since they could the more readily find him and show him to others in their sacred writings, inasmuch as he was really in them; and since they manifested as great an aversion for sensuous representations, or at all events were shown in these Scriptures as possessing an aversion as great as the Persians had always felt; it is not surprising that they found favour in the eyes of Cyrus with a divine worship which he recognized as being, no doubt, far below pure Sabeism, but yet far above the rude idolatries which in its stead had taken possession of the land of the Jews.

40. Thus enlightened respecting the treasures which they had possessed without knowing it, they returned, and became quite another people, whose first care it was to give permanence to this enlightenment amongst themselves. Soon apostasy and idolatry among them was out

of the question. For it is possible to be faithless to a national deity, but never to God, after he has once been recognized.

41. The theologians have tried to explain this complete change in the Jewish people in different ways; and one, who has well demonstrated the insufficiency of these explanations, wanted finally to give, as the true reason—"the visible fulfilment of the prophecies which had been spoken and written respecting the Babylonian captivity and the restoration from it." But even this reason can only be true in so far as it presupposes the exalted ideas of God as they now are. The Jews must now, for the first time, have recognized that to do miracles and to predict the future belonged only to God, both of which powers they had formerly ascribed also to false idols; this precisely is the reason why miracles and prophecies had hitherto made so weak and fleeting an impression upon them.

42. Doubtless the Jews became better acquainted with the doctrine of immortality among the Chaldeans and Persians. They became more familiar with it, too, in the schools of the Greek philosophers in Egypt.

43. However, as this doctrine did not correspond with their Scriptures in the same way that the doctrines of God's unity and attributes had done—since the former were entirely overlooked by that sensual people, while the latter would be sought for: and since too, for the former, previous exercising was necessary, and as yet there had been only *hints* and *allusions*, the faith in the immortality of the soul could naturally never be the faith of the entire people. It was and continued to be only the creed of a certain section of them.

44. An example of what I mean by "previous exercising" in the doctrines of immortality, is the divine threat of punishing the misdeeds of the father upon his children unto the third and fourth generation. This accustomed the fathers to live in thought with their remotest posterity, and to feel in advance the misfortunes which they had brought upon these innocents.

45. What I mean by an "allusion" is something which might merely excite curiosity, or call forth a question. As, for instance, the common figure of speech which describes death by "he was gathered to his fathers."

46. By a "hint" I mean something which contains some sort of germ, from which the truth which up to now has been held back, may be developed. Of this character was the inference of Christ from God's

title as "the God of Abraham, Isaac, and Jacob."[1] This hint appears to me to be undoubtedly capable of development into a strong proof.

47. In such exercises, allusions, hints, consists the *positive* perfection of a primer; just as the above-mentioned quality of not putting difficulties or hindrances in the way to the truths that have been withheld, constitutes its *negative* perfection.

48. Add to all this the clothing and the style.

(1) The clothing of abstract truths which could scarcely be passed over, in allegories and instructive single circumstances, which were narrated as actual occurrences. Of this character are creation in the image of growing day; the origin of evil in the story of the forbidden tree; the source of the variety of languages in the story of the tower of Babel, etc.

49. (2) The style—sometimes plain and simple, sometimes poetical, throughout full of tautologies, but of such as call for a sharp wit, since they sometimes appear to be saying something else, and yet say the same thing; sometimes seem to say the same thing over again, and yet to mean or to be capable of meaning, basically, something else:—

50. And there you have all the good qualities of a primer both for children and for a childlike people.

51. But every primer is only for a certain age. To delay the child, that has outgrown it, longer at it than was intended, is harmful. For to be able to do this in a way which is at all profitable, you must insert into it more than there is really in it, and extract from it more than it can contain. You must look for and make too much of allusions and hints; squeeze allegories too closely; interpret examples too circumstantially; press too much upon words. This gives the child a petty, crooked, hairsplitting understanding: it makes him full of mysteries, superstitious, full of contempt for all that is comprehensible and easy.

52. The very way in which the Rabbis handled *their* sacred books! The very character which they thereby imparted to the spirit of their people!

53. A better instructor must come and tear the exhausted primer from the child's hands—Christ came!

54. That portion of the human race which God had wished to embrace in one plan of education, was ripe for the second great step.

---

[1] Matt. xxii. 32. In the fourth fragment of 1777 Reimarus denies the validity of Jesus' argument (Lachmann-Muncker, xii, pp. 395–97).

He had, however, only wished to embrace in such a plan that part of the human race which by language, habits, government, and other natural and political relationships, was already united in itself.

55. That is, this portion of the human race had come so far in the exercise of its reason, as to need, and to be able to make use of, nobler and worthier motives for moral action than temporal rewards and punishments, which had hitherto been its guides. The child has become a youth. Sweetmeats and toys have given place to an awakening desire to be as free, as honoured, and as happy as its elder brother.

56. For a long time, already, the best individuals of that portion of the human race had been accustomed to let themselves be ruled by the shadow of such nobler motives. The Greek and Roman did everything to live on after this life, even if it were only in the memories of their fellow-citizens.

57. It was time that another *true* life to be expected after this one should gain an influence over the youth's actions.

58. And so Christ was the first *reliable, practical* teacher of the immortality of the soul.

59. The first *reliable* teacher. Reliable, by reason of the prophecies which were fulfilled in him; reliable by reason of the miracles which he achieved; reliable by reason of his own revival after a death by which he had put the seal to his teaching. Whether we can still *prove* this revival, these miracles, I put aside, as I leave on one side *who* the person of Christ was. All *that* may have been at that time of great importance for the first acceptance of his teaching, but it is now no longer of the same importance for the recognition of the *truth* of his teaching.[1]

60. The first *practical* teacher. For it is one thing to conjecture, to wish, and to believe in the immortality of the soul, as a philosophic speculation: quite another thing to direct one's inner and outer actions in accordance with it.

61. And this at least Christ was the first to teach. For although, before him, the belief had already been introduced among many nations, that bad actions have yet to be punished in the life to come; yet they were only such actions as were injurious to civil society, and which had, therefore, already had their punishment in civil society too. To preach an inward purity of heart in reference to another life, was reserved for him alone.

[1] Cf. the end of *On the Proof of the Spirit and of Power.*

62. His disciples have faithfully propagated this teaching: and even if they had had no other merit than that of having effected a more general publication among other nations of a truth which Christ had appeared to have destined for the Jews alone,[1] yet if only on that account, they would have to be reckoned among the benefactors and fosterers of the human race.

63. If, however, they mixed up this one great truth together with other doctrines whose truth was less enlightening, whose usefulness was less considerable, how could it be otherwise? Let us not blame them for this, but rather seriously examine whether these very commingled doctrines have not become a new directing impulse for human reason.

64. At least, it is already clear from our experience that the New Testament Scriptures, in which these doctrines after some time were found preserved, have afforded, and still afford, the second, better primer for the race of man.

65. For seventeen hundred years past they have occupied human reason more than all other books, and enlightened it more, were it even only through the light which human reason itself put into them.

66. It would have been impossible for any other book to become so generally known among such different nations: and indisputably, the fact that modes of thought so completely diverse from each other have turned their attention to this same book, has assisted human reason on its way more than if every nation had had its *own* primer specially for itself.

67. It was also most necessary that each people should for a time consider this book as the *non plus ultra* of their knowledge. For the youth must believe his primer to be the first of all books, so that his impatience to be finished with it may not hurry him on to things for which he has not yet laid the foundations.

68. And that is also of the greatest importance now. You who are cleverer than the rest, who wait fretting and impatient on the last page of the primer, take care! Take care that you do not let your weaker classmates notice what you are beginning to scent, or even see!

69. Until these weaker fellows of yours have caught up with you, it is better that you should return once more to this primer, and examine

[1] Here the influence of Reimarus is apparent. Coleridge's marginal comment is: "How was it possible that Lessing could assert this in the face of 'Go ye into all nations'? Cf. the discourse with the Samaritan woman etc. etc."

whether that which you take only for variations of method, for superfluous verbiage in the teaching, is not perhaps something more.

70. You have seen in the childhood of the human race, in the doctrine of the unity of God, that God makes immediate revelations of mere truths of reason, or has permitted and caused pure truths of reason to be taught, for a time, as truths of immediate revelation, in order to promulgate them the more rapidly, and ground them the more firmly.

71. You learn in the childhood of the human race the same thing, in the doctrine of the immortality of the soul. It is *preached* in the second, better primer as revelation, not *taught* as a result of human reason.

72. As we by this time can dispense with the Old Testament for the doctrine of the unity of God, and as we are gradually beginning also to be less dependent on the New Testament for the doctrine of the immortality of the soul: might there not be mirrored in this book also other truths of the same kind, which we are to gaze at in awe as revelations, just until reason learns to deduce them from its other demonstrated truths, and to connect them with them?

73. For instance, the doctrine of the Trinity. How if this doctrine should in the end, after countless waverings to one side or the other, merely bring human reason on the path to recognizing that God cannot possibly be One in the sense in which finite things are one, that even his unity must be a transcendental unity which does not exclude a sort of plurality? Must not God at least have the most perfect conception of himself, i.e. a conception which contains everything which is in him? But would everything be contained in it which is in him, if it contained merely a conception, merely the possibility even of his necessary reality, as well as of his other qualities? This possibility exhausts the being of his other qualities. Does it exhaust that of his necessary reality? I think not. Consequently either God can have no perfect conception of himself at all, or this perfect conception is just as necessarily real (i.e. actually existent) as he himself is. Admittedly the image of myself in the mirror is nothing but an empty representation of me, because it only has that of me which is reflected by rays of light falling on its surface. If, however, this image contained everything, everything without exception, which is contained in me, would it then still be a mere empty representation, or not rather a true double of myself? When I believe that I recognize in God a similar reduplication,

I perhaps do not so much err, as that my language is insufficient for my ideas: and so much at least remains for ever incontrovertible, that those who want to make the idea acceptable to the popular intelligence could scarcely have expressed themselves in a more apt and comprehensible form than by giving the name of a Son whom God begets from eternity.[1]

74. And the doctrine of original sin. How if finally everything were to convince us that man, standing on the first and lowest step of his humanity, is by no means so much master of his actions that he is *able* to obey moral laws?

75. And the doctrine of the Son's satisfaction. How if everything finally compelled us to assume that God, in spite of that original incapacity of man, chose rather to give him moral laws, and forgive him all transgressions in consideration of his Son, i.e. in consideration of the living embodiment of all his own perfections, compared with which, and in which, all imperfections of the individual disappear, than *not* to give him those laws, and thus to exclude him from all moral bliss, which cannot be conceived of without moral laws?

76. Let it not be objected that speculations of this nature upon the mysteries of religion are forbidden. The word mystery signified, in the first age of Christianity, something quite different from what it means now: and the development of revealed truths into truths of reason, is absolutely necessary, if the human race is to be assisted by them. When they were revealed they were certainly not truths of reason, but they were revealed in order to become such. They were like the "facit" said to his boys by the mathematics master; he goes on ahead of them in order to indicate to some extent the lines they should follow in their sums. If the scholars were to be satisfied with the "facit," they would never learn to do sums, and would frustrate the intention with which their good master gave them a guiding clue in their work.

77. And why should not we too, by means of a religion whose historical truth, if you will, looks dubious, be led in a similar way to closer and better conceptions of the divine Being, of our own nature, of our relation to God, which human reason would never have reached on its own?

78. It is not true that speculations upon these things have ever done

[1] For the argument see *The Christianity of Reason*, (below, p. 99). Here Lessing says nothing of the Spirit.

harm or been injurious to civil society. Reproach is due, not to these speculations, but to the folly and tyranny which tried to keep them in bondage; a folly and tyranny which would not allow men to develop their own thoughts.

79. On the contrary, though they may in individual instances be found wanting, speculations of this sort are unquestionably the most fitting exercises of the human reason that exist, just as long as the human heart, as such, is capable to the highest degree of loving virtue for its eternal blessed consequences.

80. For this selfishness of the human heart, which wishes to exercise its understanding only on that which concerns our bodily needs, succeeds in blunting rather than in sharpening it. It is absolutely necessary for it to be exercised on spiritual objects, if it is to attain its perfect illumination, and bring out that purity of heart which makes us capable of loving virtue for its own sake alone.

81. Or is the human species never to arrive at this highest step of illumination and purity?—Never?

82. Never?—Let me not think this blasphemy, All Merciful! Education has its goal, in the race, no less than in the individual. That which is educated is educated for a purpose.

83. The flattering prospects which are opened to the youth, the honour and well-being which are held out to him, what are they more than means of educating him to become a man, who, when these prospects of honour and well-being have vanished, shall be able to do his *duty*?

84. This is the aim of *human* education, and does the divine education not extend as far? Is nature not to succeed with the whole, as art succeeded with the individual? Blasphemy! Blasphemy!

85. No! It will come! it will assuredly come! the time of the perfecting, when man, the more convinced his understanding feels about an ever better future, will nevertheless not need to borrow motives for his actions from this future; for he will do right because it *is* right, not because arbitrary rewards are set upon it, which formerly were intended simply to fix and strengthen his unsteady gaze in recognizing the inner, better, rewards of well-doing.

86. It will assuredly come! the time of a new eternal gospel, which is promised us in the primers of the New Covenant itself![1]

[1] Revelation xiv. 6.

87. Perhaps even some enthusiasts of the thirteenth and fourteenth centuries had caught a glimmer of this new eternal gospel, and only erred in that they predicted its arrival as so near to their own time.

88. Perhaps their "Three Ages of the World" were not so empty a speculation after all, and assuredly they had no bad intentions when they taught that the new covenant must become as antiquated as the old has become. There remained with them the same economy of the same God. Ever, to put my own expression into their mouths, ever the selfsame plan of the education of the human race.

89. Only they were premature. They believed that they could make their contemporaries, who had scarcely outgrown their childhood, without enlightenment, without preparation, at one stroke men worthy of their *third age*.

90. And it was just this which made them enthusiasts. The enthusiast often casts true glances into the future, but for this future he cannot wait. He wants this future to come quickly, and to be made to come quickly through him. A thing over which nature takes thousands of years is to come to maturity just at the moment of his experience. For what part has he in it, if that which he recognizes as the best does not become the best in his lifetime? Does he come again? Does he expect to come again? It is strange that this enthusiasm is not more the fashion, if it were only among enthusiasts.

91. Go thine inscrutable way, Eternal Providence! Only let me not despair of thee because of this inscrutableness. Let me not despair of thee, even if thy steps appear to me to be going backward. It is not true that the shortest line is always straight.

92. Thou hast on thine eternal way so much that thou must concern thyself with, so much to attend to! And what if it were as good as proved that the great, slow wheel, which brings mankind nearer to its perfection, is only set in motion by smaller, faster wheels, each of which contributes its own individual part to the whole?

93. It is so! Must every individual man—one sooner, another later— have travelled along the very same path by which the race reaches its perfection? Have travelled along it in one and the same life? Can he have been, in one and the selfsame life, a sensual Jew and a spiritual Christian? Can he in the selfsame life have overtaken both?

94. Surely not that! But why should not every individual man have been present more than once in this world?

95. Is this hypothesis so laughable merely because it is the oldest? Because human understanding, before the sophistries of the Schools had dissipated and weakened it, lighted upon it at once?

96. Why may not even I have already performed all those steps towards my perfection which merely temporal penalties and rewards can bring man to?

97. And, once more, why not all those steps, to perform which the prospects of eternal rewards so powerfully assist us?

98. Why should I not come back as often as I am capable of acquiring new knowledge, new skills? Do I bring away so much from one visit that it is perhaps not worth the trouble of coming again?

99. Is this a reason against it? Or, because I forget that I have been here already? Happy is it for me that I do forget. The recollection of my former condition would permit me to make only a bad use of the present. And that which I must forget *now*, is that necessarily forgotten for ever?

100. Or is it a reason against the hypothesis that so much time would have been lost to me? Lost?—And what then have I to lose?—Is not the whole of eternity mine?

VI

THE CHRISTIANITY OF REASON[1]

1. The one most perfect Being has from eternity been able to be concerned only with the consideration of what is the most perfect thing.

2. The most perfect thing is himself; and thus from eternity God has only been able to contemplate himself.

3. To conceive, to will, and to create are one with God. One can therefore say that anything which God conceives he also creates.

4. God can think only in two ways: either he thinks of all his perfections at once, and of himself as inclusive of them all, or he thinks of his perfections individually, one separated from another, and each one by itself in its own grade.

5. God contemplated himself from eternity in all his perfection; that is, God created from eternity a being lacking no perfection which he himself possessed.

6. This being is called in Scripture the Son of God, or, which would be still better, the Son-God. A God because he lacks none of the attributes which belong to God. A Son because according to our ideas that which conceives a thing has a certain priority to the conception.

7. This being is God himself and is not to be distinguished from God because one thinks of it as soon as one thinks of God, and one cannot think of it without God; that is, because one cannot think of God without God, or because that would be no God at all from whom one would take away his own conception.

8. This being one can call an image of God, indeed an identical image.

9. The more two things have in common with one another, the

[1] *Lessings Werke*, ed. Lachmann-Muncker, xiv, pp. 175–8. This fragment was found among Lessing's papers and published by his brother in 1784. Lessing probably made these notes about 1752–53, occasioned by reading J. W. Hecker's *Christentum der Vernunft* (1752). They show the immense influence on his mind of Leibniz's ideas about the Great Chain of Being. That Lessing took this kind of speculative theology seriously is shown by the similar argument in *The Education of the Human Race*, § 73.

greater is the harmony between them. Therefore the greatest harmony must exist between two things which have everything in common with each other, that is, between the things which together are only one.

10. Two such things are God and the Son-God, or the identical image of God; and the harmony which exists between them is called by Scripture *the Spirit which proceeds from the Father and Son.*

11. In this harmony is everything that is in the Father and also therefore everything that is in the Son; this harmony is therefore God.

12. But this harmony is God in such a way that it would not be God if the Father were not God and the Son were not God, and that both could not be God unless this harmony existed; that is, *all three are one.*

13. God contemplated his perfections individually, that is, he created beings each one of which has something of his perfections; for, to repeat it once again, every thought is a creation with God.

14. All these beings together are called the World.

15. God could think of his perfections divided in an indefinite variety of ways. There could therefore be an indefinite number of possible worlds were it not that God thinks always of the most perfect, and thus amongst all these thought the most perfect of worlds, and so made it real.

16. The most perfect way of thinking of his perfections individually is that of thinking of them individually in infinite grades of greater and less, which so follow on one another that there is never a jump or a gap between them.

17. Therefore the beings in this world must be ordered in such grades. They must form a series in which every member contains everything that the lower members have, and something more; but this something never reaches the final limit.

18. Such a series must be an infinite series, and in this sense the infinity of the world is incontestable.

19. God creates only simple things, and the complex is a secondary consequence of his creation.

20. Since each of these simple beings has something which the others have, and none can have anything which the others have not, there must be a harmony among these simple beings; and from this harmony everything may be explained that happens among them, that is, in the world.

21. To this point at some future time a fortunate Christian will extend the sphere of natural philosophy, but only after long centuries when explanations have been found for all phenomena in nature so that there is nothing left to do except trace them to their true origin.

22. Since these simple beings are as it were limited gods, their perfections also must be similar to the perfections of God, related as parts to the whole.

23. To God's perfections belong also the consciousness of his perfection and the power to act according to his perfections; both are as it were the seal of his perfections.

24. With the various grades of his perfections must therefore be connected various grades of the consciousness of these perfections and the power to act in accordance with them.

25. Beings which have perfections, which are conscious of their perfections, and which have the power to act in accordance with them, are called moral beings, that is beings which can follow a law.

26. This law is derived from their own nature, and can be none other than: *Act according to your individual perfections.*

27. Since in the series of beings there cannot possibly be a jump, there must also exist beings which are not sufficiently clearly conscious of their perfections. . . .

VII

ON THE REALITY OF THINGS OUTSIDE GOD[1]

However I may seek to explain the reality of things outside God, I must confess that I can form no idea of it.

If it is called "the complement of possibility,"[2] I ask: Is there in God an idea of this complement of possibility or not? Who will assert that there is not? But if the idea of it is in him, then the thing itself is in him: all things are real in him.

But, it will be said, the idea which God has of the reality of a thing does not do away with the reality of this thing outside him. Does it not? This reality outside him must have something which distinguishes it from the reality in his idea. That is: in the reality outside him there must be something of which God has no idea. An absurdity! But if there is nothing of the sort; if in the idea which God has of the reality of a thing everything is present that is to be found in the reality outside him, then both realities are one, and everything which is supposed to exist outside God exists in God.

Or it may be said: The reality of a thing is the sum of all possible definitions that may be applied to it.[3] Must not this sum also be in the idea possessed by God? What definition has the reality outside him if the ideal is not present in God? Consequently this ideal is the thing itself, and to say that the thing also exists outside this ideal means that this ideal is duplicated in a way both unnecessary and absurd.

I believe that when philosophers say they affirm the reality of a thing outside God, they mean nothing more than the mere assertion that this thing is different from God, and its reality is to be explained in another way from the necessary reality of God.

But if this is all they mean, why should we not say that the ideas which God has of real things are those real things themselves? They are

[1] Lachmann-Muncker, xiv, pp. 292–3. The fragment was written about 1763, and first printed by Karl Lessing in 1795.

[2] This is the language of Christian Wolff, the popularizer of Leibniz.

[3] The definition comes from Alexander Baumgarten's *Metaphysica*.

still sufficiently distinct from God, and their reality becomes in no sense necessary because they are real in him. For must not the contingency which they must have outside him also correspond to an image in his idea? And this image is merely their contingency itself. What is contingent outside God is also contingent in God, or God could not have any idea of the contingent outside him. I use this phrase "outside him" as it is commonly used, to show from the way I apply it that it ought not to be used.

But people will cry out in horror: Contingencies in the immutable being of God! Why? Am I the only one who does this? You yourselves must ascribe to God ideas of contingent things. Has it never occurred to you that ideas of contingent things are contingent ideas?

VIII

ON THE ORIGIN OF REVEALED RELIGION[1]

1. To acknowledge one God, to seek to form the ideas most worthy of him, to take account of these most worthy ideas in all our actions and thoughts, is the most complete summary of all natural religion.

2. To this natural religion every man, according to the capacity of his powers, is committed and bound.

3. But since this capacity differs with every man, and accordingly each man's natural religion will be different, it has been thought necessary to guard against the disadvantages which this difference can cause not in the state of man's natural freedom but in the state of his social connection with other people.

4. That is: as soon as it is recognized as a good thing to make religion a concern for the community, people must be united about certain things and ideas, and to attribute to these conventional things and ideas precisely the importance and necessity which the acknowledged truths of natural religion possess in their own right.

5. That is: out of the religion of nature, which was not capable of being universally practised by all men alike, a positive religion had to be constructed, just as out of the law of nature, for the same cause, a positive law has been constructed.

6. This positive religion received its sanction through the distinction of its founder, who claimed that the conventional elements in it came from God, only mediated through him, just as certainly as the essential elements in it were immediately derived from God through each individual's reason.

7. The indispensability of a positive religion, because of which the natural religion is modified in each State according to its natural and

---

[1] Lachmann-Muncker, xiv, pp. 312–13, first published by Karl Lessing in 1784 from his brother's papers. Muncker dates the fragment in Lessing's Breslau period, 1763–64, but Witkowski (*Lessings Werke*, vi, p. 428) thinks it earlier, probably about 1755.

accidental conditions, I call its inner truth, and this inner truth is as great in one as in another.

8. Consequently all positive and revealed religions are equally true and equally false.

9. Equally true: in so far as it has everywhere been necessary to come to an agreement over various things in order to get uniformity and unity in public religion.

10. Equally false: in that the matters on which agreement is reached not only stand beside what is essential but also weaken and supplant it.

11. The best revealed or positive religion is that which contains the fewest conventional additions to natural religion, and least hinders the good effects of natural religion. . . .

IX

THE RELIGION OF CHRIST, 1780[1]

"For the Father also seeketh those who thus worship him."
St. John

1. It is a question whether Christ was more than a mere man. That he was a real man if he was a man at all, and that he never ceased to be a man, is not in dispute.

2. It follows that the religion of Christ and the Christian religion are two quite different things.

3. The former, the religion of Christ, is that religion which as a man he himself recognized and practised; which every man has in common with him; which every man must so much the more desire to have in common with him, the more exalted and admirable the character which he attributes to Christ as a mere man.

4. The latter, the Christian religion, is that religion which accepts it as true that he was more than a man, and makes Christ himself, as such, the object of its worship.

5. How these two religions, the religion of Christ and the Christian religion, can exist in Christ in one and the same person, is inconceivable.

6. The doctrines and tenets of both could hardly be found in one and the same book. At least it is obvious that the former, that is the religion of Christ, is contained in the evangelists quite differently from the Christian religion.

7. The religion of Christ is therein contained in the clearest and most lucid language.

8. On the other hand, the Christian religion is so uncertain and ambiguous, that there is scarcely a single passage which, in all the history of the world, has been interpreted in the same way by two men.

[1] *Lessings Werke*, ed. Lachmann-Muncker, xvi, pp. 518–19.

BIBLIOGRAPHY

The following list is selective, and gives the titles of works found useful in the making of the present volume.

ANER, K. *Die Theologie der Lessingzeit*, 1929.

ARX, A. VON. *Lessing und die geschichtliche Welt*, 1944.

BARTH, K. *Die protestantische Theologie im 19. Jahrhundert*, 1947.

CASSIRER, E. *Die Philosophie der Aufklärung*, 1932 (= *The Philosophy of the Enlightenment*, 1951).

DILTHEY, W. *Das Erlebnis und die Dichtung*, 8th ed., 1922.

EICHHOLZ, G. "Die Geschichte als theologisches Problem bei Lessing," *Theologische Studien und Kritiken*, cvii (1936), pp. 377–421.

FITTBOGEN, G. *Die Religion Lessings*, 1923.

GARLAND, H. B. *Lessing, the Founder of Modern German Literature*, 1937.

HAZARD, P. *La Pensée européenne au XVIIIᵉ Siècle: de Montesquieu à Lessing*, 1946 (= *European Thought in the Eighteenth Century*, 1954).

HIRSCH, E. *Geschichte der neuern evangelischen Theologie*, iv, 1952.

KOFINK, H. *Lessings Anschauungen über die Unsterblichkeit und Seelenwanderung*, 1912.

LOOFS, F. "Lessings Stellung zum Christentum," *Theologische Studien und Kritiken*, lxxxiii (1913), pp. 31–64.

SCHMIDT, E. *Lessing*, 2nd ed., 1899.

SCHNEIDER, H. *Lessing: Zwölf biographische Studien*, 1951.

SIME, J. *Lessing*, 1877.

STEPHAN, H. "Lessing und die Gegenwart," *Zeitschrift für Theologie und Kirche*, N.F., x (1929), pp. 401–434.

STRAUSS, D. F. *Hermann Samuel Reimarus und seine Schutzschrift für die vernünftigen Verehrer Gottes*, 1862.

THIELICKE, H. *Vernunft und Offenbarung*, 1936.

TRAUB, F. "Geschichtswahrheiten und Vernunftswahrheiten bei Lessing," *Zeitschrift für Theologie und Kirche*, N.F., i (1920), pp. 193–207.

WAGNER, A. M. "Who is the Author of Lessing's 'Education of Mankind'?" *Modern Language Review*, xxxviii (1943), pp. 318–27.

WALLER, M. *Lessings Erziehung des Menschengeschlechts*, 1935.

WERNLE, P. *Lessing und das Christentum*, 1912.

ZSCHARNACK, L. *Lessing und Semler*, 1905.

INDEX

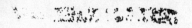